SCHIZOPHRENIA

Examines the nature of this illness, how it affects the
sufferers and their families, and what can be done to help.

SCHIZOPHRENIA
A guide to what it is and
what can be done to help

Jacqueline M. Atkinson Ph.D.

THORSONS PUBLISHING GROUP

First published August 1985
This revised edition published 1989

British Library Cataloguing in Publication Data

Atkinson, Jacqueline M.
Schizophrenia. — Rev. ed.
1. Man. Schizophrenia
I. Title
616.89'82

ISBN 0-7225-1990-7

*Published by Thorsons Publishers Limited, Wellingborough,
Northamptonshire NN8 2RQ, England*

Printed in Great Britain by Mackays of Chatham, Kent

3   5   7   9   10   8   6   4   2

CONTENTS

To those sufferers and their families whom I have met and worked with, especially those in the Glasgow Branch of the National Schizophrenia Fellowship, and who have taught me so much. Without them this book could never have been written.

FOREWORD

Imagine a disease which strikes down the great majority of its sufferers just as they are poised to enter the prime of their lives, which ruptures the close, complex relationship between the emotional and intellectual functioning of their minds, which leaves them psychologically crippled and precariously vulnerable to life's most mundane stresses and which does not distinguish between class nor creed nor educational attainment, and you begin to have some awareness of the problem of schizophrenia. Whether it is one disease or a constellation of syndromes is not known. Nor is it known what causes it nor how it might be cured. What is known is that schizophrenia is not rare — about as many people suffer it as suffer from diabetes — and its terrible impact, not merely on those affected directly by it, but on families and friends is recognized to be, in the main, a catastrophic one.

For those who are stricken by schizophrenia, and for their immediate families, the widespread ignorance and misconceptions about the condition are just one more agony to be suffered. The tendency of thoughtless journalists and careless politicians to equate 'schizophrenic' with 'in two minds', 'uncertain', 'mercurial', 'contradictory' and 'like Jekyll and Hyde' would not in itself matter very much but the complete misunderstanding of what is actually involved in this psychotic illness reflects a widespread public apathy and indifference. But the ignorance is not limited to the general public. Many health care professionals, including general practitioners, social workers, health visitors and district nurses whose work brings them into regular contact with schizophrenic patients and their families in the community, have but the haziest idea of the nature and effects of schizophrenia, of the treatments used, of the problems associated with maintenance and relapse in the community and of the possibilities of treatment.

This book is explicitly written for sufferers and their families and, by virtue of its lucidity of expression and absence of tiresome obfuscation and jargon, it is certain to be of immense assistance and, indeed, reassurance. But professionals, too, can read it with profit and particularly its second section where the trials and strains of patients and their families are poignantly and accurately outlined. At the present time, schizophrenia can be controlled but not cured. Our treatments, while strikingly effective compared with former days, are still inadequate for eliminating the root cause. Thus it is even more important that every effort is made to ensure that the plight of sufferers and their relatives is lessened to the greatest possible extent that current knowledge permits. This book is a substantial contribution to the easing of this plight, and patients, relatives and those who are privileged to treat individuals who are suffering have reason to be grateful to the author.

PROFESSOR ANTHONY CLARE

INTRODUCTION

At the outset of his or her schizophrenia both the sufferer and their family may be distressed and frustrated by the apparently cavalier fashion in which their requests for information are treated. What is it? What causes it? How long will it last? Will he be able to go back to work? When? Will he relapse? If so, when? And what do we do? When will he be better? What is the cure? How do I cope? How do we cope? Why us? Why *me*?

There are no absolute, foolproof answers to these questions. In fact there are few, if any, complete answers at all and anyone who tells you they have *the* answer, be it to cause, cure, management or anything else, is lying. That is the bad news.

The good news is that we do have *some* information, *some* tentative answers and some ideas about management. Sadly this is rarely shared or used in the most sensible and appropriate way. Families who have lived for years with the problem know the day-to-day difficulties much better than even the most eminent consultant psychiatrist. Many have learnt, by a process of trial and error, the best way to deal with their problems. Sharing these experiences could help many other families just starting out on the struggle.

Individuals are all different and so are families, so there is no *one* answer, no answer that applies to everyone. This book does not pretend to be definitive; it cannot possibly cover all eventualities, be they problems or solutions. It is simply a beginning, covering the areas which, in my experience, are most important; sharing suggestions, experiences, explanations and trying to bring some cohesion out of chaos.

Part One of the book sets the background, and is an attempt to answer basic questions about what schizophrenia is and what happens once it is diagnosed, including treatment and care. Part

Two turns to the more pressing practical problems of living with schizophrenia and dealing with the problems this presents, to sufferers, families and friends.

Since schizophrenia affects more males than females I use the masculine pronoun for the sufferer, simply for ease of expression, but the comments apply equally to male and female sufferers.

PART I
BACKGROUND

1.

WHAT IS SCHIZOPHRENIA?

The first important question anyone is likely to ask on being told of the diagnosis of schizophrenia is 'What *is* it?'. Most people will know that it is a mental illness, but no more than that. Or, maybe even worse than nothing, their ideas are wrong and totally misleading. Even a patient who *knows* what is happening to him, who may even have some understanding of his problems, may still want to know 'But what is *schizophrenia*? Is that really what I have got?' Feelings of fears and anxiety often occur in both sufferer and relative when the diagnosis is made plain, sometimes accompanied by hostility or even denial.

It is important to understand what schizophrenia is, its symptoms and how they affect the individual. This helps the sufferer to gain some perspective on his own experience, and gives his family and friends some understanding of what is going on. Without knowing something about the central aspects of schizophrenia, how they make the sufferer behave, little success will be made of management.

Schizophrenia as Psychosis

Psychiatric disorders can be classified into two main groups, the neuroses and psychoses. Neuroses are the more common and include emotional and behavioural problems. Generally most people can understand the symptoms or problems the person has and can, by and large, empathize with them. Psychoses, on the other hand, are the more serious illnesses. The symptoms are not easily understood by others and most people cannot empathize with them. The patient often loses contact with reality and frequently does not know that he is ill, the problems being defined by others. The psychoses are further divided into organic or functional categories. The organic psychoses are those in which an organic or biological cause can be shown, such as a tumour, changes in blood supply, infections, toxic factors, traumas (accidents) or congenital factors. In the functional psychoses there is disturbance in the functioning of the individual, but no organic cause can be shown. Positive symptoms (described below) need to be clearly shown. There are two main functional psychoses: affective or manic depressive psychoses and schizophrenia.

Symptoms

When we talk about schizophrenia, we are not dealing with one discrete entity, but more likely with a group or spectrum of disorders. This means that not all sufferers will show exactly the same symptoms, nor will they have the same kinds of experience. Nevertheless, there is a group of symptoms which are considered to be central, or the 'core' of schizophrenia, and the individual must exhibit some of these to qualify for the diagnosis of schizophrenia.

For schizophrenia to be diagnosed with confidence at least some of the following symptoms must be present.

1. Disorders of thought

This concerns the form of thinking as well as the content of the thoughts. The distinction is important, and disturbance in the *way* the individual thinks is as important as *what* he thinks in making the diagnosis.

A. *Disturbances in the form of thought*

There is no definition of formal thought disorder which is generally acceptable. The term applies to a number of types of problems in thinking and also in speech and thus communication. Thinking is generally woolly, vague and diffuse, and speech, to the listener, seems disjointed and incoherent. Such disturbances must be clear, and must display an inability to be explained by 'normal' means, such as extreme emotion, difficulties with thinking, comprehension or communication due to limited intelligence, limited education, language problems or cultural differences. The last two are particularly important for immigrant groups for whom English is a foreign language. Thinking impaired by drugs or alcohol would not be applicable.

i) *Associations*

One area of disorder in the form of thinking concerns the relationship between words, the associations that the person makes. Thus the person may make unusual or non-logical associations. For example, common associations to the word 'cat' might be 'dog/mouse/mat'. The logical connection is clear and understood by everybody. An unusual response might be 'apple', where there does not seem to be any logical connection. This, obviously, can lead to difficulty in understanding the speech of the individual if it happens a lot. It may be experienced as 'Knight's move' thinking — an expression taken from chess. The thinking is not 'straight' but turns a corner and, unless the listener knows what this is, the sequence of ideas being expressed seems incomprehensible. Sometimes the person is able to explain the seeming illogicality (e.g. they had recently seen a cat stuck up an apple tree being rescued by the owner) but at other times they may not have an explanation, or only be able to produce one which is unacceptable to the listener (e.g., an explanation in terms of a delusion or bizarre belief).

The odd association made may be of several common types. Thinking may be over-inclusive, that is, groups of things are expanded until usual or logical connections are lost, and the connections are then used inappropriately. Again if time is taken, some reason for the connection may become apparent. For example, a saw, screwdriver and hammer will be seen as a logical group by most people, as would a saw, hatchet and axe. In neither group would one usually expect to see included a set of dentures. Although they can be regarded as a useful tool (as in group one of general tools) or even a specific tool for cutting (group two) the association strikes the listener as bizarre.

Another type of association commonly made is the clang association, that is, the words rhyme. Some rhyming is acceptable, and usually has a common meaning or association, e.g. of 'the cat sat on the mat' type, but others seem to have no sense behind them. Sometimes the individual's 'sentence' may be no more than a string of rhyming words.

ii) *Concrete thinking*
The individual has difficulty, or is even unable to think in abstract terms. Analogies are not understood, nor are metaphors. This is best demonstrated by asking for the meaning of a well-known proverb; for example, 'a stitch in time saves nine' will only be explained in terms of sewing, knitting and mending. This may affect the appreciation and understanding of humour, sarcasm and irony as remarks are taken literally.

iii) *Grammatical distortions*
Grammar may be used in idiosyncratic ways, including the ordering of parts of speech and changes in their use.

iv) *Poverty of speech*
Replies are stereotyped, that is, the same response is given to each question (e.g. 'I don't know') or the same response is given repeatedly over time, even when circumstances have changed. This category also includes general vagueness and lack of detail in speech.

v) *Autistic thinking*
Reasoning is disturbed by personal ideas, themes or associations intruding into the rational or logical sequence of thought. This will be influenced by the content of thought and the experience of delusions or hallucinations.

vi) *Disturbances of expression*
The disturbances in the form of thinking described here, as well as other symptoms, lead to difficulties in communication and expression.

(a) *'Word salad'* This describes a stream of disjointed, unrelated words and ideas, either in speech or writing, which makes no apparent sense to anybody.

(b) *Neologisms* These are 'made-up' words, used to describe or label new ideas, places, things or people and are usually related to delusions or hallucinations.

(c) *Thought blocking* This manifests in sudden halts in the thinking process, and a feeling of 'blankness'.

B. *Disorders in the content of thought*
This refers primarily to delusions, but insight is also included.

i) *Delusions*
A delusion is a false belief which is held by the individual, is

unacceptable to everybody else (i.e., is regarded as 'wrong') and cannot be shaken by reason, argument or demonstration. The influence of culture is especially important here and care should be exercised to exclude beliefs held by different cultures or cultural sub-groups. The belief may be transitory, in that it is not maintained, or only maintained during acute periods or relapse, or it may be sustained over long periods of time and become an habitual part of the way the person sees the world. The individual's behaviour may, or may not, be influenced by his delusional beliefs.

Delusions may appear in two ways, being seen as primary and secondary.

(a) *Primary delusions* — These appear suddenly, in a fully developed form, and the patient accepts them immediately. This is usually related to delusional perception (see below).

(b) *Secondary delusions* — These usually arise more slowly, and out of other symptoms. They are generally the attempts of the patient to 'explain' other problems or symptoms. For example, thought disorder may be explained by the belief that someone is trying to control him, or rays from the television interfere with his brain. Or the primary belief in being controlled may lead to a delusional belief in the activities of the CIA/KGB/MI5/men from Mars and so forth.

The possibilities for delusional belief are limitless, and include such phenomena as simple ideas of grandiosity and persecution. Although usually associated with schizophrenia they neither occur in all schizophrenics, nor are limited to schizophrenia. Emphasis in diagnosis is placed on particular categories. These are:

(a) *Delusional perception* — This is of exceptional diagnostic significance. The individual attributes a special, highly personal significance to a routine, normal, innocuous perception in the absence of any reasonable justification for so doing. The significance of the event is usually both overwhelming in its importance and is urgent. For example, the person may believe that because he sees a car signal and then turn right, this means that he has a special mission to save the world from its own folly. These delusions are almost always primary in that they occur suddenly and totally and are instantly accepted. The individual will then usually try to act in accordance with the new belief.

(b) *Thought insertion* — The individual experiences thoughts which he feels have been literally put into his head by an outside agent or agency. Such thoughts are not experienced as 'his' but belong to another. This may be used to 'explain' strange thoughts the individual is experiencing.

(c) *Thought withdrawal* — The person experiences losing thoughts or feels that they are being taken away, removed from his mind without his co-operation by an external agent. Again, this may be used to 'explain' strange happenings in the thought process.

(d) *Thought broadcast* (thought diffusion) — Thoughts are being broadcast to others in some way by an external agent, again without his co-operation.

(e) *Delusions of control* — These will be discussed under disturbances of volition rather than thinking.

(f) *Ideas of reference* — Everyday normal events are perceived normally, but they are seen as having special importance for the individual and may be related to delusional perception.

ii) *Insight*

The individual usually lacks insight into his condition, frequently refusing to acknowledge that there is anything wrong at all. Others may say there is something wrong, but the patient sees the problem as being with the others, often other family members, rather than themselves, e.g., relatives or friends are seen as intolerant, not understanding or deliberately misunderstanding. Or the problems may be explained in terms of one of the systems of delusional beliefs.

2. Disturbances of perception

The main area of concern here is with hallucinations, but attentional problems also need consideration.

A. *Hallucinations*

These can occur in many other illnesses, but are usually associated with clouded consciousness (for example, in a fever, through alcohol or other drugs). In schizophrenia they are experienced whilst the individual has clear consciousness. An hallucination is the experience of something without appropriate, relevant or adequate sensory stimulation. This simply means that the person sees or hears something when there is nothing there (to another observer) to create the picture or sound. Any of the senses may be involved, the most common being hearing.

i) *Auditory hallucinations*

The person hears things that no one else does. It is important that the sounds (usually voices) are experienced in the way we usually hear voices — that is, they are heard outside the head, rather than as ideas spoken aloud in the mind. Auditory hallucinations can take several forms.

(a) *Audible thoughts* — The individual hears their thoughts spoken aloud, by another voice.

(b) *Voices conversing* — Voices are heard in conversation, talking about the individual in the third person. For example, 'He doesn't look very happy today, does he? What do you suppose is the matter?'

The voices may make all kinds of remarks about the person which may or may not be true, and may make suggestions about him that are particularly disturbing, e.g. 'John is really a homosexual, but he will not admit it'.

(c) *Voices commenting* — One or more voices describe the person's behaviour, or comment on it, as it happens; asides may be added. For example, 'Now she is getting out the shopping bags. She is putting on her coat. She must be going out.'

In any of these circumstances the voices may only comment and talk away to themselves, or they may address the person directly.

ii) *Visual hallucinations*

These may accompany auditory hallucinations, giving the voices form; or things or people may be seen that are not physically there, or things may appear distorted.

iii) *Tactile hallucinations*
The sufferer feels things that are not occurring. He might experience painful sensations in parts of his body, or other unpleasant sensations, for example a crawling under the skin as though he is infested with maggots.

iv) *Olfactory hallucinations*
The person smells something that no one else can. They might experience their own body odour, or that of others, as particularly unpleasant.

3. Disorder of attention

The individual experiences severe problems in concentration: in attending to what is happening in the outside world, to tasks that he is trying to accomplish, or even to his own thoughts. This may be secondary to another problem, e.g. thought disorder, delusions or hallucinations, or it may simply seem to arise for no particular reason. It can make the accomplishment of anything extremely difficult and, at times, hazardous.

4. Disorder of volition

There is often a general loss of motivation, with the individual appearing to have no willpower to do anything, lack of drive and being generally apathetic. In some cases the person may exhibit excessive obstinacy or automatic obedience.

A. *Somatic passivity*
This may be experienced as an hallucination, in that the individual is being interfered with in his functioning by some outside force or agency.

B. *Alien control*
The sufferer experiences his thoughts, feelings, motor acts and impulses as either imposed by an external force or controlled from outside his body. The feelings, impulses or acts carried out are described as being 'made to do something'. The person has little control over what he does, or only has control in some areas.

C. *Negativism*
The person does the opposite of what he is asked to do, or sometimes what he intends to do.

5. Motor disorder

A. *Catatonia*
This is a rare category. In its extreme form the person may hold rigid positions, usually of a bizarre nature, for long periods of time. Waxy flexibility, where the person can be moved into other positions may also occur and, rarely, echopraxia, where the sufferer automatically repeats the actions of others.

B. *Mannerisms and posturing*
Mannerisms are strange, highly stylized movements, generally idiosyncratic to the patient, usually having a special meaning or purpose. For example the person may need to make a series of movements before sitting down or entering a room, or may get up and repeatedly circle his chair. Odd hand movements and gestures may be apparent, odd or poorly co-ordinated movement, posture and gait may be seen, as may grimacing and strange facial movements. In the case of the latter group of movements care should be taken to exclude the possibility of drug side-effects.

6. Disorder of emotion
An early sign is often seen as lack of rapport at the interview stage.

A. *Flat affect*
Here affect means emotion, and the individual is seen to be 'flat' emotionally. This is sometimes called blunting of affect. No emotion is expressed, the person's features do not express feelings, and they seem generally apathetic rather than calm.

B. *Emotional incongruity*
This affects only a small number of sufferers, but is an important feature of hebephrenia. The mood or emotion displayed is inappropriate or incongruous with the situation or the individual's thoughts. For example, someone might laugh whilst telling you how unhappy they are.

7. Disturbances in interpersonal relations
These problems can be either secondary, as a result of the foregoing symptoms, or part of the individual's premorbid (i.e. before the onset of the illness) personality. Many sufferers have a history in which withdrawal from social situations, an inability to get on with others and isolation form a large part. For others withdrawal seems to reflect their inability to deal with reality as

it is, in the face of their own experiences, such as delusions, hallucinations and thinking problems.

These symptoms do not all appear at once, and will not all occur in the one patient. Onset may be slow or sudden and this affects the picture presented. There are a number of different sub-types of schizophrenia which emphasize different sorts of symptoms. There is a growing tendency not to use these in diagnosis now, as it is not always easy to distinguish them. Before these are discussed, however, brief mention must be made of another division in schizophrenia. The primary, florid symptoms may disappear, but the sufferer may be left with other problems. The stages of schizophrenia may be broadly divided into two, acute and chronic. Not everyone develops the problems of chronic schizophrenia, but when these symptoms do develop they can be as debilitating as the acute, florid symptoms.

Acute Schizophrenia
In the acute phase of schizophrenia the symptoms, as previously described, occur in their most dramatic or florid form. It is during this stage that schizophrenia can be diagnosed most clearly, either at first breakdown or as a relapse. The sufferer is very ill, usually out of touch with reality for much of the time, possibly with no, or little, insight. Hospital admission is usually necessary, for both observation and treatment. Drugs are the most effective form of treatment we have at present, and in the majority of patients they bring the florid symptoms under control. (This will be discussed further in Chapter 5.)

Chronic Schizophrenia
The chronic condition often follows the acute stage of schizophrenia and is characterized by the presence of negative symptoms, such as flattened affect, withdrawal and lack of motivation. Sometimes these are referred to as secondary symptoms, resulting from the sufferer's response to the acute symptoms. In some cases, however, these may precede the acute attack. These symptoms produce other problems, often described as residual disability, such as difficulty in getting on with other people, problems in working and looking after oneself, general isolation and apathy. The distinction is not entirely clear-cut, and there is some degree of overlapping. For example, delusional

thinking or hallucinations may persist through the chronic stage, although often in a less dramatic form than the acute stage.

The variety of difficulties encountered in the chronic stage are many and varied and include the responses of the sufferer and others to the illness as well as the symptoms themselves. It is these additional handicaps, and the circumstances in which the sufferer finds himself, that contribute to the wide range of problems presented by sufferers and families and for which little help is given.

Sub-types of Schizophrenia

It is more useful to see the sub-types of schizophrenia as ways of classifying schizophrenic reactions and symptoms rather than as discrete clinical entities. There are four classic sub-types.

1. Paranoid schizophrenia

The most typical symptoms are primary and secondary delusions, usually of persecution, accompanied by auditory hallucinations. Onset is likely to be later in life than other types, between the mid-twenties and fifty.

Usually of a fairly high intelligence, the paranoid schizophrenic is suspicious from the outset and misinterprets everyday things, events and the reactions of others, usually in a way that is negative to himself, although some of the delusions may have a grandiose content. Feelings of persecution may arise from the misinterpretation of others' actions, but will also lead to misinterpretation. Paranoid symptoms usually take a chronic course, but the individual's personality may remain fairly intact, i.e. he still seems 'normal' most of the time. If the delusions remain 'encapsulated' the sufferer may behave normally in most circumstances and only in special conditions will his strange beliefs be seen. Generally, however, the delusional beliefs will cause him to have some conflict with society over his beliefs or behaviour resulting from them. The premorbid personality may often show paranoid traits, including hypersensitivity or extreme self-consciousness, where offence is taken at harmless remarks. The common stereotypes of this sub-group are the person who thinks he is Napoleon (delusion of grandeur) or the person who thinks MI5/KGB/'everyone' is out to get him (persecution).

2. Hebephrenic schizophrenia

Since the onset of hebephrenia is usually in the late teens, early symptoms may be dismissed as typical adolescent difficulties. Such problems, however, are more severe, persistent and deep rooted. Early symptoms include poor concentration, moodiness, excessive day-dreaming, perplexity and confusion, self-consciousness, feelings of inadequacy and inferiority, depression, apathy, strange ideas and preoccupation with pseudo-scientific, pseudo-philosophical or religious topics and transient behaviour. Thought disorder becomes increasingly obvious and important. Characteristic of this sub-type is emotional incongruity. The patient often sits and giggles to himself for no apparent reason. The hebephrenic is more confused and less able to function normally than the paranoid. Delusions are more likely to be grandiose than in paranoia, but the sufferer is usually less likely to want to demonstrate the validity of any delusions than the paranoid person.

3. Catatonic schizophrenia

This is an uncommon sub-type, having decreased in incidence over the last thirty years or so. The first stage may be acute excitement characterized by agitation and apparently aimless, but constant, behaviour. The sufferer then slows down, showing stereotyped behaviour, negativism, posturing and withdrawal until a state of total passivity, immobility or stupor is reached. Posturing at this stage may lead the individual to resemble a bizarrely-arranged statue, and the sufferer will remain in this position for hours or days until someone moves him. At this stage the sufferer is unable to care for any of his physical needs. There is apparent total detachment from reality, the sufferer can be told distressing information and show no reaction. Many patients, however, at the end of the catatonic episode, are aware of what they have been told and may then experience emotion. Delusions and hallucinations may be present, but during this stage the sufferer is unable to communicate these ideas, which may be of cosmic quality, e.g., 'the world is about to be destroyed'.

4. Simple schizophrenia

Unlike the previous types, simple schizophrenia does not have a sudden or dramatic onset, nor many of the florid, bizarre symptoms. It develops slowly over a period of years, usually starting during adolescence and progressively deteriorating. It may be impossible to date onset and many cases are not diagnosed or only at a late stage. The primary symptoms of schizophrenia are unusual, the condition being characterized by the sufferer becoming more and more isolated and inactive. Being unable to take part in many aspects of living, these people do not develop emotionally, socially or intellectually. Undiagnosed and alone they may drift downwards in social terms, 'dropping out', drifting into poverty or vagrancy. Living with their family or in a sheltered environment they may function better, but are unlikely to be confident or take the initiative for doing things.

Two other categories may be useful to consider and they appear increasingly as a diagnosis.

5. Schizophrenic defect state
This is the typical picture of chronic schizophrenia. It is the negative symptoms which predominate, and the general picture is one of poverty of emotion, thought and motivation, withdrawn, eccentric behaviour and isolation.

6. Schizo-affective disorder
This is a category which seems to be used more in recent years than the past, particularly in America. It is often used when doubt exists about the diagnosis between schizophrenia and the affective psychoses. Some schizophrenic symptoms appear to be present, but there is a strong emotional content, possibly including depression. The acute phases may be shorter than in schizophrenia, but relapses are to be expected.

Understanding the Symptoms
These, then, are the symptoms of schizophrenia, the things for which the psychiatrist is looking when making a diagnosis. Most of these symptoms are unknown to those of us who are not schizophrenic and are difficult, sometimes impossible, to comprehend or imagine.

For example, many will understand the concept of 'voices' — that the schizophrenic individual is hearing a voice, or voices, that other people do not. But can we really understand what this means and what the problems that arise from this phenomena really are? Possibly the hearer will be aware that something is not quite right, and that no one else hears the voices. This may come about because of the nature of the voices, what they are saying, the fact that no one else responds to them, or he makes reference to them and they are denied by everyone else. Yet still he hears them. Clearly someone's perception is at fault. Who is he to believe? His family and friends who, until this point, he may have always trusted and had faith in? But that would be to deny his own senses, what he *knows* is happening. He cannot believe both, one or other have to be denied. What would *you* do?

Then there is the physical problem of the sound. Any conversation he has with others, any thoughts he tries to concentrate on, any programme he tries to listen to on the television or radio, is heard against a background noise of voices talking to him, or talking about him. Some sufferers experience the voices intermittently, but others hear them constantly, a continual intrusion of sound against which everything else takes place.

The problem of the constant noise can be aggravated and made more stressful by the content of the commentary or overheard conversation. The sufferer has no control over this and may be exposed to things which are painful, embarrassing or shocking. The voices may talk about violence or sex in a manner which is upsetting, particularly if they suggest that the sufferer may want to take part in acts which he considers perverted. They may challenge basic beliefs and assumptions the person holds about himself, suggesting, for example, that he is really homosexual, or hates his parents. Whilst the individual may know this to be untrue, constant repetition of such statements can bring their own doubts with them and, as well as adding to stress and anxiety, can produce self-doubts, loss of confidence and feelings of insecurity.

While all of this is happening, the person experiencing it may desperately be trying to hide it from his family and friends. Maybe if he ignores it, it will go away — or at least so he hopes. How can you begin to explain an experience like this to anyone? Especially, how can you convince them of its reality, that it is not imagination? And how can you convince them without being told that you are mad? This is a crucial dilemma. Not all sufferers are aware that what is happening to them is unusual, but those that are fear for their sanity. This fear can prevent them seeking help at an early stage, prevents them telling anyone what is going on or what is worrying them. It is this fear which is possibly the greatest burden of all.

As I have already said, the symptoms of schizophrenia are not easily understood by the non-schizophrenic. Hearing voices is one of the most dramatic symptoms that it is possible to try to understand, but others are much more difficult. The vagaries of thought disorder, for example, are so complex and unusual as to defy normal comprehension. Moreover, I would strongly suggest that though you try to understand the problem, and how it affects the sufferer, you *do not* try to experience it yourself in any way. The experiences you may succeed in achieving may not always be easily dispersed.

A way to aid understanding is to read some of the books written by schizophrenic individuals about their experiences. Some examples are given at the end of the book, under 'Further Reading'. But the indiosyncracies of the schizophrenic experience must always be borne in mind: what happens for one person is not necessarily true for another. I have not mentioned discussing the symptoms with the sufferer himself in terms of his own experiences for the very good reason that this can be a difficult, dramatic and sometimes dangerous task. This whole issue will be discussed in Chapter 7.

2.

THE DIAGNOSIS
OF SCHIZOPHRENIA

What is a Diagnosis?

The meaning of diagnosis comes in two parts. The most commonly understood meaning is simply that it is a term which denotes the disease or illness from which a person suffers. So, for example, measles, coronary thrombosis and cerebral haemorrhage are all diagnoses of what is wrong with an individual. So is schizophrenia.

The second meaning of diagnosis is, to quote *The British Medical Dictionary*, 'The art of applying scientific methods to the elucidation of the problems presented by a sick patient'. This means that information about the person and the condition must be collected, sifted, analysed and evaluated critically to arrive at a diagnosis. Most importantly, it means that this evidence for disease should come from every available source including biological, psychological and social factors and all possible methods should be used to collect it.

Why Diagnose?

By combining all the information we can from individual patients, with what we already know about the body (or mind), we can learn more about the illness as a whole, what causes it, and how it affects the patient. This serves three purposes. It may enable the disease to be put in a certain recognized category of diseases. Amongst other uses this can then provide statistics of illness trends which are important in planning for the provision of health care services. Much more importantly for the individual, however, it tells us how to approach the treatment of an individual patient and what the prognosis (the course and outcome of the disease) is likely to be.

Some people object to the use of diagnoses, seeing them merely as labels which dehumanize the problem. Doctors, it is suggested, must deal with 'problems' in all their multifaceted, unclassifiable, messy glory and not simply aim to 'treat disease'. The suggestion is that labelling a condition is not only useless, but does positive harm, especially in the mental illnesses. This is usually because of the social stigma attached to the label and the concept of hopelessness that is often connected to this. In part this is true. There is a tendency, not only amongst doctors, for the diagnosis, the disease label, to take over. Thus the person is not spoken of as an individual suffering from schizophrenia, but becomes 'the schizophrenic'.

Few would want to contradict these valid points and they represent a humane, concerned and caring approach both within and outside the medical profession. It is, however, a case which can be overstated. Diagnosis *is* important. As has been mentioned, treatment depends on it. If this is *all* the doctor uses though, his help may be limited. Of course other factors are relevant: each individual brings with him a unique set of personal and social factors which must be taken into account and, in some cases, help must be provided to deal with other problems arising from these. But if the diagnosis is not made, then the help given can often only be general and possibly superficial. To be either too narrow, and look at diagnosis and nothing else, or too broad and abandon the concept of labels altogether, can both severely impair the competence of the doctor or other professional caregiver.

Who Makes the Diagnosis?

The diagnosis is the responsibility of the psychiatrist. He may ask for, and gather, information from various other groups, including nurses, social workers and psychologists; but making the final diagnosis lies firmly within the province of the medical profession.

What is the Psychiatrist Looking for When He Makes the Diagnosis?

Basically, the psychiatrist is looking for certain types of symptoms that are specific to a particular diagnostic class, in this case schizophrenia. He is also looking for the absence of other types of symptoms or conditions which might account for the symptoms which are observed. As mentioned in the previous chapter there are certain cardinal or core symptoms which must be present. These are usually referred to as first-rank symptoms and comprise thought insertion, thought withdrawal, thought broadcasting, feelings of passivity, voices heard talking about the patient in the third peson, voices arguing, voices heard speaking aloud the patient's own thoughts, primary delusions, made feeling, made impulses and made volitions. If several of these are present then the diagnosis can be made with confidence.

How is the Diagnosis of Schizophrenia Made?

The diagnosis of schizophrenia is a clinical diagnosis, that is, there are no physical tests that can be carried out to give a definite answer. Blood tests, X-rays, brain scans and the like cannot be used to diagnose schizophrenia. In some cases physical examinations may be needed to rule out other possibilities, but there is no need to assume negligence if this is not done. In most instances it is not necessary.

How then, does the psychiatrist get his information? On what does he base his diagnosis? Broadly, information of three kinds is collected.

1. A 'present state' description — This is simply what it says. The psychiatrist interviews the patient, often more than once, talking to him, asking him questions, letting him express what he is thinking, feeling and experiencing. The aim of this is to find out whether the patient is displaying any of the signs or symptoms of illness, to evaluate this, and to see if there is any evidence of abnormal behaviour, thoughts, feelings or experiences.

2. A clinical history — This might include such factors as whether there have been previous episodes of illnesses, when and how they were treated and how the patient responded, and types of symptoms previously experienced.

3. Other information — This will tend to be information concerning possible causes, pathology or problems. Included here will be results of laboratory tests, if any have been carried out, and response to specific types of treatment if this has already been started.

Other types of information routinely collected include a full personal history covering such areas as birth and childhood, education, social development and behaviour, sexual development and behaviour, and work history. Often a family history is also asked for, especially any history relating to mental illness.

When all of this information is collected together it is analysed more or less consciously by applying a set of classifying rules to arrive at a particular diagnostic category.

The Diagnostic Interview

How does the psychiatrist decide what symptoms are present? Three major factors influence his judgement: the type of interview he employs, his definition of symptoms, and the way in which the patient responds.

There are 'standard' interviews which the psychiatrist may follow, but they are not the same as a test or questionnaire and they simply standardize the interviews between patients. They are useful in allowing for comparison, as well as standardizing the procedure of the interview. There also needs to be an agreed set of descriptions or definitions of the symptoms under consideration.

The patients' responses require careful consideration. Do the patient and psychiatrist mean the same thing regarding the symptoms? The technique of cross-examination is usually employed. The doctor will have in mind a certain symptom and will ask a series of questions to determine whether the patient has that symptom. Each question is determined by the response of the patient to the previous question. A symptom is not rated as present simply because the patient says he has it. This method of interviewing is flexible enough to allow for individual variation in responses, but still allows for a common set of issues to be dealt with. It does, however, require expert and experienced clinicians.

Doubtful Diagnosis

As can be seen from this explanation of the diagnosis of schizophrenia it is not a wholly straightforward procedure, and there are no absolute rules or tests. For most people there will be a general consensus of opinion: 'Yes, this person has schizophrenia' or 'no, he does not'. For a few though, there will be doubt and confusion. Particularly in the early stages it may be difficult to make a firm diagnosis. Other information, such as the patient's premorbid personality or family history, may give some support to a diagnosis, but usually it is the observation of the progress of the condition over time which finally clarifies the diagnosis.

This can mean that it may be some time before a diagnosis is given to either the patient or the family. Whilst this can cause some worry, most people would agree that it is safer to err on the side of caution and not 'label' someone too quickly on insufficient evidence. Indeed, there are some psychiatrists now who will only use the diagnosis of schizophrenia at the second episode of acute symptoms. They argue that its recurring nature is part of the illness and of diagnostic importance. Obviously this means that the sufferer will not be told of a diagnosis at first breakdown. The psychiatrist may suspect schizophrenia but will not convey this to the patient or his family.

Negative Diagnostic Findings
When making the diagnosis negative findings play an important part. Various other disorders must be excluded, particularly manic and depressive symptoms, organic dementia and epilepsy. There may be causes other than schizophrenia which account for some of the symptoms and these must also be excluded, particularly alcohol abuse, drug use and abuse and organic lesions. It must be distinguished from normal adolescent problems and psychological difficulties. Where the individual is particularly shy, sensitive, self-conscious and intelligent this may pose particular problems.

What Schizophrenia is Not
There is confusion in the minds of much of the public about what schizophrenia is. Sometimes it is as important to explain what it is *not* as to describe what it is. A schizophrenic is not simply someone who is bad or whom you do not understand, or who is weak and inadequate, or violent and unpredictable. Nor is schizophrenia related to the psychological difficulties of normal adolescence. It is not a 'bad trip' or related to drug or alcohol abuse. It has no connection with subnormality or mental handicap; and it is most definitely *not* split personality. There is a very rare condition of dual or multiple personality, but this has nothing to do with schizophrenia. There might be mood and other changes in the behaviour of the schizophrenic sufferer, one

day pleasant the next not, or sometimes friendly, sometimes withdrawn, but this is not the same as split personality.

What is the Prognosis?

Prognosis means no more than what is likely to happen in the future. This involves the probable course of the illness as well as the probable outcome. It is based on all the relevant facts, which include a wide variety of factors relating to the individual seen in relation to experience and the knowledge of how these have affected outcome in previous cases.

There is not a simple prognosis in schizophrenia. Roughly twenty per cent of sufferers 'recover' or at least are in remission without treatment. About two-thirds achieve some sort of recovery with treatment which means they will spend most of their time out of hospital, only becoming in-patients at times of relapse. The extent to which they live 'normal' lives, however, is highly variable. Whereas in the past over sixty-six per cent of sufferers spent their lives in hospital care, today the number is less then ten per cent. Although a chronic illness, schizophrenia is not fatal, unless through suicide. This only applies to a tiny number of cases.

What Factors Affect Prognosis?

Some factors, not part of the illness, point to a favourable outcome. These include no family history of schizophrenia, a normal premorbid personality, normal social development, a stable family background and relationships and a normal work record. In terms of features of the illness those associated with a good outcome include acute onset, precipitating factors, the retention of a normal emotional response, drive and initiative and the presence of catatonic elements.

Outcome is also affected by treatment, early treatment assisting a favourable prognosis. Treatment plays an important part in relapse rates, possibly making the intervals between relapses longer. This will be discussed further in later chapters.

Onset

A little more needs to be said about onset. Where this is rapid, possibly as quickly as an overnight deterioration into an acute episode, the prognosis tends to be favourable, even when the symptoms are very bizarre. This is especially true if the attack is preceded by an event which is obviously stressful to the individual. This could range from the death of a family member to work problems. This only holds true if the event cannot be related to the illness. So, for example, problems at work which have been caused by the person behaving peculiarly do not count. Rapid onset tends to go with good pre-illness adjustment, both personaliy and socially.

Onset can, however, be slow and insidious. The person's functioning and behaviour are affected over a long period of time, gradually becoming more and more incapacitating. Generally the person has always had some sort of problem and may have been especially shy and sensitive, withdrawing from social contacts and spending time alone. In bright adolescents this can be masked to some extent by them working very hard and achieving good academic results — at least until the problem gets out of control. An onset of this type has a less favourable outcome, the individual tending to remain chronically disabled.

3.

WHOM DOES SCHIZOPHRENIA AFFECT?

The answer is a surprisingly large number of people are affected by schizophrenia, especially when those affected indirectly are also included in the calculations. Obviously it is the sufferer, the patient, who is directly affected and it is usually only these who are counted. There are, however, important indirect effects on family and friends.

Directly — the Sufferer
A rough estimate suggests that throughout the world one person in every hundred will suffer from schizophrenia at some time in their lives. This is a staggeringly high number and from the outset I hope you will be able to take some comfort in knowing that you, either as a sufferer or as a relative are not alone, that you are one of a large group of people.

Not everyone who develops the illness is ill at the same time though. At any one moment some people will be acutely ill, others will be chronically ill, and yet others will be in a stage of remission, well and functioning normally, or at least fairly normally.

One of the problems with the diagnosis of 'schizophrenic' is that once the individual has been labelled as such he tends to be stuck with it for life. Although a proportion go into a remission stage and seem not to have any more acute attacks, few are pronounced 'cured'. So although there may not have been a relapse or acute phase for many years, the label tends to persist. This is particularly sad since the illness tends to strike young. The majority of sufferers develop the condition during their teenage and young adult years, between sixteen and thirty, so it becomes a label for life.

This young age of onset itself contributes to secondary problems, such as unfinished education or job training, lack of social contacts and social life and general under-confidence in the adult role. Schizophrenia is not, however, exclusively a condition of the young and some middle-aged and elderly people do develop symptoms (of the paranoid type in particular).

Who develops schizophrenia?

I have already said that schizophrenia tends to strike young. It is more common in males than females. The sufferer is usually of at least average intelligence, but the individual's capacity or motivation to make use of his intellectual ability may well be affected, and thus the sufferer may not appear as bright as he really is.

The incidence of schizophrenia, that is, the occurrence of new cases in the population, suggests that it is not necessarily tied to particular groups in terms of class, occupation or race. The prevalence of schizophrenia, that is the frequency of the disease in the population, however, ties it to the lower social classes, inner city living, unskilled occupations and related factors. This probably has more to do with the course of schizophrenia than anything else. As the sufferer's problems persist and they find it increasingly difficult to stay in work for which they were trained or suited, they will, where possible, take jobs of a lower level. It may be that they are unable to work at all. So they are said to 'drift down the social scale'. This is complicated by the fact that accommodation for single people, or those on low, fixed incomes is usually easier to find in inner city areas. Hostels and sheltered housing tend to be centred there, also contributing to the gathering of chronic sufferers together in 'ghettos' in the poorer inner areas.

The 'career' of the schizophrenic patient

Factors affecting individual prognosis, and thus career, are important and these were considered in the previous chapter. There are, nevertheless, broad outlines for areas in the sufferer's life which will be affected.

Hospital career

Almost all sufferers will find themselves in hospital at some time or other. Roughly fifteen to twenty per cent of admissions to psychiatric hospitals have a diagnosis of schizophrenia. In terms of the hospital population as a whole this means that approximately forty-five per cent of the patients are diagnosed as schizophrenics. When the long-stay patients are considered as a group then the majority, over eighty per cent, will be suffering from chronic schizophrenia. What happens during a stay in hospital, the treaments involved and what happens after discharge are set out in the chapter on treatment and care.

Social career
Much here depends on the sufferer's pre-morbid personality. If this has been good and his social development normal, then with some help and understanding from his family and friends and some determination on his part he should be able to take up the reins of his social life. This will not be, usually, without some problems, and adverse reactions from friends will increase any tendency to withdrawal. Nevertheless, where the sufferer has a network of friends and social contacts to return to the possibility for maintaining them can be high.

More problems exist where the pre-morbid personality was poor and the individual was already fairly withdrawn and isolated. His recovery is likely to be less complete than in the previous group and this in itself causes problems in trying to establish a social life or make new friends. Along with this the sufferer may express no desire to meet people, and may even actively avoid it, thus becoming more isolated.

If the individual had his first breakdown at a young age he may be into his middle twenties before he feels able to, or wants to, be involved with other people. If he has little or no experience of making friends and going out socially, it may then prove very difficult. Practice during teenage years in making friends, forming close relationships and simply being social and involved with others is crucial, and such skills are often difficult to acquire later without some outside, professional help.

Work career
Everything that has been said about the sufferer's social career applies equally, if not more so, to his work career. The older the person is before he gets a job the more difficult it is, not only to *get* a job, but to then be able to adjust enough to *keep* it.

The present climate of high unemployment affects the issue in two important ways. On the one hand, employers have, usually, a lot of choice when filling jobs and therefore may not even want to consider someone with a poor work record through illness, especially when it is something as little understood as schizophrenia. On the other hand, there are increasing numbers of people reaching their early twenties who have either never worked or have done so only intermittently. It is thus easier to 'hide' in this group when presenting for employment, or even when out of work. Amongst the present number of unemployed you are no longer unusual, odd or in need of long explanations for your circumstances.

Indirectly — the Family
So, the general finding is that approximately one per cent of the population is directly affected by schizophrenia and becomes a sufferer. If we consider relatives — parents, spouses, siblings, children and so on — then the numbers indirectly affected by the illness are astronomical.'

The effect on the family will vary, in part as a result of the course and severity of the illness in the patient, but also depending on the relationship involved and the family's expectations, tolerance, ability to cope and the support *they* receive. What may be a major problem for one family, e.g. coping with the sufferer talking to voices, may be easily tolerated by another, who are more upset by his lack of personal cleanliness.

This variation in problems and toleration of them can itself cause difficulties. Professionals may think they are giving help but still not deal with what is most important to the family they are trying to help. It means that every case must be approached on its own merits and analysed independently and this takes time and effort.

Rather than go into details here the problems the family faces will be discussed in detail in Chapter 8.

Indirectly — Society
Most people will consider schizophrenia's effect on society in terms of the burden imposed financially in caring for such people, in supporting those who are unable to work and in loss of production from those unable to hold down a job. It seems to me that the effect goes beyond this.

Most people do not know what schizophrenia is; they have only a vague understanding of the term and its problems. They often do not want to know and prefer to push the problem (along with the mentally retarded, physically handicapped, the aged and other 'problem groups') out of their minds (or into big mental hospitals out in the country). I believe that part of our task is not just to deal with the individual sufferer, whether as a sufferer yourself, a relative or a professional, but to face the wider issues of public education, forcing if necessary, society as a whole to face up to its responsibilities to such groups. Ultimately society itself will benefit, becoming richer as the bounds of what is accepted as 'normal' are stretched to include people who think differently, or look different, or act differently. The more rigid society becomes in defining what is 'normal' the more outsiders there will be; and one day they will outnumber the rest.

4.

WHY?

When either you, or someone in your family, is given the diagnosis of schizophrenia a question which will quickly follow on from 'What is it?' is 'Why?' All sorts of why. Why me? Why us? Why now? How has it happened? What causes it?

What Causes Schizophrenia?
No one really knows what causes schizophrenia. The best we can say is that there is a strong possibility that certain factors are implicated in its cause. Doctors talk about the aetiology of schizophrenia, which simply means the factors which cause it. There is, as far as we know at the moment, no one factor that can be held responsible for causing schizophrenia. Most people would agree that schizophrenia needs several factors to combine in one individual to produce the illness.

There are four main areas to look at when considering theories of the causation of schizophrenia — genetic factors, biochemical factors, the environment and the family. It is difficult to separate these factors in many instances and their importance may depend on factors interacting rather than having an effect on their own. Each of these four areas will be considered in turn.

Genetic Factors
It is generally agreed that genetics play a part in schizophrenia. But how this works is not yet properly understood.

Genes are the means by which physical and mental characteristics of the parents are passed on to the children. The genes themselves are not all equal in their ability to pass on characteristics and therefore the process is an extremely complex one and may involve more than one gene for a particular characteristic. In some characteristics, for example colour of eyes, we know how the process works, but in others, for example schizophrenia, we do not.

It has already been mentioned that the incidence of schizophrenia is one in one hundred. This means that for the general public the lifetime risk of schizophrenia is one per cent. However, when we look at families which have a schizophrenic member, we find that the likelihood of other first degree family members (mothers, fathers, brothers, sisters) is much higher, about ten times higher (ten per cent risk). For second degree relatives (uncles, aunts, nieces, nephews, grandparents, grandchildren and half-brothers or sisters) the risk is three times higher (three per cent) than the general population. The child of a schizophrenic parent (either mother or father) has a risk of nearly fifteen per cent of developing schizophrenia which rises to forty per cent if both parents are schizophrenic. The highest risk, however, is found between identical twins, when it reaches fifty per cent. For non-identical twins the rate is higher than for a brother or sister, about seventeen per cent. Thus it can be seen that the closer the blood relationship, the greater the chance of developing schizophrenia if you have a schizophrenic relative.

These figures are guidelines only; a full family history of both parents would be needed to be more specific. Although the blood relationship links suggest that schizophrenia might be inherited, there is also the possibility of a shared environment playing a part. Much of the evidence for the heritability of schizophrenia comes from the study of twins. Since identical twins come from one fertilized egg their genetic make-up is identical. If the development of schizophrenia depended on genetic factors alone then the risk for schizophrenia would be one hundred per cent for an identical twin with a schizophrenic twin. As the rate is not this high it means that whilst a genetic factor is likely to be present and important, it does not account for the entire cause of schizophrenia.

More evidence for the genetic aspects of schizophrenia comes from adoption studies. Children born to schizophrenic mothers, but brought up away from the mother and away from the mother's family, had a higher risk factor for schizophrenia than children from non-schizophrenic mothers adopted away from their families.

Although the data suggest that there is a genetic link in the development of schizophrenia, this does not mean that a person is born schizophrenic. Rather the individual is born with the predisposition to develop schizophrenia, and why or how this may happen is discussed under Environmental Factors, below.

Biochemical Factors

The general assumption is that the genetic factors which predispose the individual to schizophrenia act through the individual's body chemistry. Thus biochemical imbalance affects the individual's brain in some way. Despite a great deal of research being carried out in this area there is no overwhelming evidence for a specific biochemical abnormality. Again, all we have is probabilities. The theory which has the most support at the moment involves dopamine.

Dopamine is a chemical which is found in the brain, a neurotransmitter, and which conducts messages in the brain. The brain has receptors which dopamine latch on to. There is some evidence that the brains of schizophrenic patients have too many receptors for dopamine, which causes an overload of dopamine and hence, eventually, a confusion of messages.

The evidence for the implication of dopamine in schizophrenia comes from several sources. Studies of people who have abused amphetamines show that many develop schizophrenia-like symptoms. Amphetamines are related to increased levels of dopamine when they are taken by non-schizophrenic individuals. Neuroleptic drugs (to be discussed further in the next chapter) which are thought to block dopamine receptors reduce the schizophrenic-like symptoms of amphetamines. A possible side-effect of neuroleptic drugs in some schizophrenic patients is the development of Parkinson-like symptoms, especially stiff posture, a mask-like facial expression and tremor. In Parkinson's disease there is a lowered level of dopamine in the brain. It can be treated by giving the patient L-dopa, which is broken down into dopamine in the body. Thus it would seem that the neuroleptics lower the level of dopamine in the brain which, in some cases, results in the Parkinsonian symptoms.

Post-mortem studies on a number of schizophrenic brains have indicated that there are increased numbers of dopamine receptors when compared to non-schizophrenic brains. However, not all those brains from people diagnosed schizophrenic had increased numbers of receptors; about one-third showed no increase. This evidence indicates that although dopamine may play a part in schizophrenia its complete role is still unknown. There is no proof that it *causes* schizophrenia, nor that it is implicated in *all* people diagnosed as schizophrenic. Neuroleptic drugs are only effective where acute symptoms are present, thus dopamine would seem to be related to these rather than to the chronic symptoms.

Environmental Factors

As has already been mentioned, various social factors are connected with schizophrenia, such as low social class, but again these are not necessarily causal. Although one theory suggests that the stresses and pressures of living in the lower social classes may be greater than in other classes and therefore can lead to more people developing schizophrenia, this seems unlikely.

Stress, however, does appear to be implicated in the development of schizophrenia. This stress may be in many forms, from the family, work or school, social pressures, and events in the person's environment or life. Family pressures and stresses will be discussed in the next section.

Stressful life events seem to be implicated in schizophrenia. Their relationship to the cause or development of schizophrenia is unclear, but there is some evidence for a relationship between life events and a schizophrenic relapse. Life events covers eventful, but essentially 'normal', changes in a person's life and includes births, deaths and marriages, changes in the family or at work, or in the person's social life. The changes need not be only those normally considered stressful, namely negative changes. Positive changes can also bring about stress. *Change* itself is the crucial factor. It seems that the schizophrenic individual is unduly sensitive to these events. The effective time link seems to be about three weeks. Where they seem implicated in relapse they are referred to as precipitating events.

Stress can also occur in other forms, and come from people rather than events or changes in circumstances. It often takes the form of pressure, to achieve something, be someone, do something. It may be that the pressure put upon the schizophrenic is not unduly high, but rather that the person with a predisposition to schizophrenia is unduly sensitive to such pressure.

Family Factors

Over the years there have been a number of theories which link schizophrenia with upbringing or various types of families. Most of these have now been discredited. There are a number of difficulties in trying to establish causal links. Even if, for example, it is shown that the family or parents' behaviour is abnormal in some way, this might well be a response to the ill individual and their bizarre behaviour rather than causing it.

One theory suggested that a particular type of mother who is over-protective, hostile and cold, unable to understand her child's feelings, might cause schizophrenia to develop in a child who was vulnerable. Other theories have suggested that it is not the mother alone who causes the problem, but that particular types of abnormal marital relationship are involved. One example, called a 'skewed' relationship, was characterized by one passive parent (frequently the father) giving way to the dominant, abnormal parent. Another type of abnormal marital relationship is the 'schism' when the two parents are in conflict, pursue their separate goals, and compete for the child's support and allegiance. Although these types of relationships may exist in the families of some schizophrenics they also occur in some families of non-schizophrenic 'normal' individuals and therefore there is no proven link between schizophrenia and abnormal types of parental relationship.

Other theories have considered communication within the family to be at the root of the problem. Probably the best-known of these is the double-bind theory. These types of communication put the child in a 'no-win' situation, as they are repeatedly given contradictory messages. The clearest example of this is the command 'Don't be so obedient', or expressing concern over the amount a person smokes whilst offering them a cigarette. Double-bind communications, where they can be identified, seem to occur in all types of families, not only those with a schizophrenic member. Again, the evidence does not link this type of communication with the development of schizophrenia.

The one area of research that is important regarding the family and schizophrenia links family behaviour, not to causing schizophrenia, but to relapse rates. This involves what is called high expressed emotion (HEE). The emotion expressed within the family towards the schizophrenic member is high and unpleasant, usually critical, but it may take the form of over-protectiveness. This seems to be experienced as a stressor by the patient, a stressor which may become intolerable. This will be discussed in more detail in Chapter 7.

Why Now?

It may be that a number of factors have come together and this has triggered the schizophrenic episode. Maybe the individual has been under considerable stress and this has proved too much for an already vulnerable person. In others there may be no apparent 'cause', no reason for this suddenly happening in someone who was previously well and happy. For yet others the acute episode may have been building up for quite some time, the person being increasingly withdrawn, moody and tense. There is no explanation why it should happen 'now' and not 'then', sooner rather than later, except to repeat that onset occurs more often in the young adult years.

Why Me?

Again, there is no one answer, or even an answer at all. It may be that you have a predisposition to become schizophrenic, possibly inherited from a family member, possibly not. It may be that there is no history of schizophrenia in your family at all and that this is something that has occurred out of the blue. There is no real answer to this question apart from saying that it is a tragic coming together of many factors.

The Search for a Cause

When something as dramatic as schizophrenia happens in a family then inevitably everyone searches for a cause; there is speculation about why this has happened, how it has happened. Parents in particular will search for a meaning in the illness, their behaviour: was it something they did or said, or did not do or say. The reasons I have heard parents suggest as causing the breakdown, or implicated in it, are as numerous as they are varied, and span the patient's entire life. They have ranged from surgery to road accidents, the birth of younger siblings to the death of a loved pet, or the way a parent has treated the child, be it rejection or smothering. It is possible that some of these might cause some behavioural problems or anxiety in a child, but alone they will not cause schizophrenia, and even in a vulnerable person they may not have had an overwhelming effect.

The important thing to remember is that it is highly unlikely that any one thing is to blame, and certainly no one person. No one deliberately sets out to create schizophrenia in a person and even if some environmental stressor seems to have triggered an episode, that alone cannot be blamed.

5.

TREATMENT AND CARE

The treatment and care of the schizophrenic patient usually takes place, in the first instance, in hospital, but may continue in other settings. We will consider here the types of treatments available, their suitability, as well as an outline of the whole 'treatment' process.

Hospital Treatment

Most schizophrenic patients at some stage will spend time in hospital. This is nothing to be either ashamed or afraid of. It is part of the course of the illness and treatment. The hospital serves three main functions for the schizophrenic individual. It is a place of safety and custody, where they will be protected from the critical harshness of the outside world and people who do not understand what is happening, and protected from themselves and their own bizarre behaviour and beliefs. Secondly, it is a place where trained people can observe what is happening and ultimately make a diagnosis. This enables the third function, treatment, to be appropriately carried out.

In-patient treatment

For many their first contact with the hospital will be at the time of the first breakdown. Where onset is sudden and dramatic the sufferer will usually be admitted to hospital straight away. Usually everyone feels relief at this as behaviour has been bizarre and frightening, both for the sufferer and relatives, none of whom understand what is happening.

Where onset is slow the sufferer may have deteriorated quite considerably before anyone realizes what is happening and hospital admission is arranged. Again there is usually a general feeling of relief on the part of both relatives and sufferers that the problem has at last been acknowledged and that something is being done.

When the schizophrenic individual's thinking has got so totally out of control that he cannot manage his own life, that he fears people and things around him, that his everyday surroundings seem alien and hostile, that simply living holds such terrors for him, then the hospital can appear a safe, protective environment. It is seen as a place where he can relinquish responsibility if he so desires, where he can begin to regain some confidence and sense of normality. For some people, however, the hospital will seem alien and threatening. This may be connected with the delusions the person experiences, so in their terms their hostility to the idea of going into hospital is reasonable, serious and not open to debate. Also the way in which someone is taken into hospital, the degree of pressure used and the amount of choice he feels he has may all contribute to make admission an unpleasant experience. Unfortunately it is those who have an unpleasant time who seem to get the most publicity and this in itself can increase the apprehensiveness of the sufferer or relatives for whom admission is a new experience.

Once in hospital there may be a period of observation before treatment begins, or medication may start almost at once. The period of in-patient treatment will be variable, depending on symptoms, response to treatment, home circumstances and individual hospital policy, but it will average six to ten weeks.

At the beginning of the stay the patient will usually be confined to the ward. Some hospitals keep everyone who is newly admitted in night clothes, some only if they think a person might actively try to leave, or simply wander away. In extreme cases of this, where the patient is so unaware of reality he might put himself in danger (or endanger others), he might be kept in a locked ward. This is not as terrifying as it sounds, and simply means the main door (to the corridor or wherever) is kept locked and the patient cannot wander about the hospital and grounds at will.

Most patients are admitted as voluntary patients and this should be encouraged whenever possible. The voluntary patient enters hospital of his own free will acknowledging that he is ill and needs help (or, at the very least, that other people think he is ill and needs help). The conditions under which a person can be committed to hospital involuntarily are encapsulated in the law of the land and are discussed in the Appendix. Generally though, patients are expected to dress during the day and will be allowed some freedom in the hospital grounds. One reason for keeping the patient close to the ward is to facilitate observation by the nursing staff, both before treatment starts and afterwards, when changes must be carefully noted.

As symptoms are brought under control the patient will be expected to take part in the various ward activities, which may cover anything from making his own bed to playing cards, to attending group therapy sessions. As improvements continue he may then spend the day away from the ward at some other unit, returning only for the evenings and to sleep. What this entails will depend on the type of hospital (a unit in a general hospital or a psychiatric hospital) and the types of facilities they have, but might include occupational, social, industrial or recreational therapy.

Out-patient treatment

On discharge from hospital the patient may be asked to continue attending as a day patient, often in the unit or day ward he has been going to for the past couple of weeks. If the hospital has no such facilities or is too far from the patient's home for him to travel in easily every day, then he might be referred to a day centre nearer his home. This is often where problems begin as there are fewer places available than people who could make use of them. If the patient has recovered well, and maintaining a job is important, then he might find himself returning straight to work.

In the majority of cases the patient will still be taking drugs. If they are of the type given by injection he will have to attend a special out-patient clinic to receive these. Often he will also be assigned a community nurse who might visit him at home, and who will check up if hospital visits are missed. Some, but not many, patients will be allocated a social worker, who will usually visit the home, often aiming to work with the family as a whole.

The psychiatrist will also expect to see the patient at an out-patient clinic for some time and this might be combined with receiving injections or prescriptions for medication. If there are any other special treatments involved, for example with a psychologist, these will continue on an out-patient basis.

The procedure at relapse is much the same and has given rise to the expression 'revolving door' policy of care. The patient is hospitalized only for short periods during an acute phase and then returned to the community for the rest of the time. The policy might result in a high number of admissions, but each will then be of a comparatively short duration; in the long run the sufferer probably still spends less time in hospital than in the past, when patients had fewer admissions but for considerably longer periods.

Community Care

You have probably heard the term 'community care' but may not be clear about what it means. Much has been written in the press and shown on television regarding community care. Much of what is shown is negative; occasionally it is startlingly good. Horror stories abound about neglect of patients in the community and ensuing tragedy. All this publicity can lead to sufferers and families being very confused about what they can, or should, expect from community care. They are not alone in this and many professionals are also confused about what community care should be.

Community care does not mean one type of treatment, or a particular service or project; rather, it should be a service tailored to meet individual needs of patients, drawing on resources from a number of agencies, including the health service, social services, housing departments, and voluntary bodies. Community care does *not*, as some people seem to think, mean care of patients *only* by their families. It *does* mean *total* care within the community. The hospital forms part of the community and must be included; so should hostels and other types of accommodation.

A visit from a community psychiatric nurse (CPN) should be part of community care, not its only manifestation. Ideally, community care should be extending its remit to include carers as well as patients, by providing services to support and educate them.

The government's policy since the 1960s has been to extend community care. During the 1980s many beds have been lost in psychiatric hospitals in the move to care for people in the community. Unfortunately, beds are disappearing before community services have been set up, and this is one of the major reasons for the problems we hear about and the difficulty in getting good services. More resources, which means more funding, are urgently needed.

If you feel that you are not getting the help you need or deserve, do not automatically assume that it is being withheld from you. More likely it does not exist in your area — or it only caters for a small number of the people who could use it.

One thing that is agreed is that where good community care projects are found they usually come from a grass roots determination to provide them. Everyone of influence, MPs, local councillors, health boards, and social work departments should be lobbied on the issue of community care. In this respect, by joining the voluntary organizations to push for, or provide, services in your area, you can do something to influence the future.

We can now turn to the specific types of treatment.

Drug Therapy

What is a drug?
In its simplest terms a drug is any substance that can interact with a biological system. This is why substances such as caffeine, nicotine or alcohol can be called drugs. The drug works by interacting with a specific site in the body, these sites being known as drug receptors.

The use of drugs in schizophrenia
The use of drugs with schizophrenic patients raises a lot of emotion in many sufferers and relatives. People from both groups are opposed to the idea of anyone having to take drugs for long periods of time, possibly even for ever. Some are opposed to drugs in principle and feel that a problem which clearly has to do with the mind should be treated in some other way than chemically, possibly by psychotherapy. Still others object to the use of drugs because of the side-effects they produce. Other relatives worry more when the patient will not take his medication, even if it has been of proven benefit in the past. Bearing all this in mind, and sympathizing with some of the points of view (particularly regarding side-effects), it is nevertheless possible to say that drugs have the most to offer the schizophrenic sufferer out of all the present treatment possibilities.

Why should this be so? As we have already considered it is more than likely that schizophrenia has, at its roots, a biochemical base, that some process in the schizophrenic's brain is not working properly. Thus, as with any other biochemical imbalance in the body, we use another chemical to try to correct this. Drugs are not the whole answer to the problem, but they do provide the best, indeed possibly the only, way of controlling the acute, primary symptoms. It is important to realize that this is not a *cure* (sadly there is no cure), but a way of 'damping down' the most florid symptoms; in some instances drugs will eliminate them altogether, in others make them less intense so that the patient can be more aware of reality. This group of drugs is referred to as neuroleptics.

Neuroleptics

The term neuroleptic means anti-psychotic. These drugs were introduced during the 1950s and their number has increased since then. Whenever medication is referred to, it almost always means these drugs. There are a number of different neuroleptic drugs, having different chemical make-up and properties, but they all seem to reduce the transmission of dopamine in the brain. This results in less acute symptoms, hallucinations, delusions and bizzare thinking. As the drugs have different chemical properties their effects on processes other than the transmission of dopamine will vary, and thus side-effects will be different. The individual's tolerance of a particular drug will also vary so it may take some time before the optimum drug in the optimum quantity can be found to control the acute symptoms, whilst having as little effect on other processes as possible. The potency of the drugs is also variable and a low dosage of one drug may be equal to a high dosage of another. So this should be checked before automatically assuming that a change in drug and dosage means the patient is getting 'more' and is therefore 'worse'. It may take anything up to three weeks for the effects of the drugs to be seen, and all that can be counselled during this time is patience.

The drugs can be given in syrup but are more usually in tablet form. Some of the neuroleptics are given by injection in depot form which simply means long-acting, the drug being stored in the body (hence depot) and released over time. This has a number of advantages, in particular the certainty that the drug has been taken. Neither sufferer nor relative has to remember on a daily basis to take or remind about drugs. The sufferer is regularly seen at the clinic, usually every one to four weeks, which means there can be consistent monitoring of side-effects and signs of a possible relapse. Some sufferers (and doctors) do not like these injections because it takes the control of taking the drug away from the sufferer. Many sufferers, however, have found them to be extremely useful.

Each of the neuroleptic drugs has one 'true' name, the generic, scientific or chemical name. This drug may be produced by different companies under their own brand or proprietary name. This might lead to some confusion if doctors refer to drugs in different ways, and you may think medication has been changed when it has not.

Phenothiazines are a group of neuroleptic drugs, and include chlorpromazine, the first widely used neuropleptic drug. Other related groups are the thioxanthenes and the chemically unrelated butyropheones. Some of the more common neuroleptics are listed in the table, together with their brand name and their recommended daily dosage.

SOME COMMON NEUROLEPTIC DRUGS

Chemical name	Brand name	Recommended daily dose (unless stated as weekly)
Chlorpromazine	Largactil Thorazine	Acute symptoms 300-900mg Maintenance dose 100-500mg
Thioridazine	Melleril	150-600mg
Trifluoperazine	Stelazine	10-20mg
Fluphenazine decanoate	Modecate	12.5-25mg every 2-4 weeks
Fluphenazine enanthate	Moditen	12.5-25mg every 1-3 weeks
Flupenthixol decanoate	Depixol	20-40mg every 1-3 weeks
Fluspirilene	Redeptin	2-8mg per week
Haloperidol	Haldol Serenace	15-200mg
Trifluperidol	Triperidol	6-8mg
Pimozide	Orap	2-20mg

Side-effects

Every drug has side-effects and the results of these must be weighed against the benefits of taking the drug. Sometimes the side-effects may be severe enough to warrant stopping the drug and switching to another type, but stopping the drugs should only be done with the psychiatrist's knowledge (and preferably consent). Most people experience nothing or little in the way of side-effects and usually find the benefits of the drug outweigh the debits.

Some side-effects are more likely with particular groups of drugs, others are possible with all neuroleptics. Some of the side-effects, such as dry mouth, constipation, drowsiness or blurring of vision, disappear or at least diminish after a few weeks' use. Drowsiness is more common with chlorpromazine (*Largactil*) than other drugs.

Most of the side-effects commonly associated with anti-psychotic drugs are those falling into the neuro-muscular category. This is the group that is thought to resemble Parkinson's disease. The patient may develop a tremor of the hands and/or feet, restlessness (akathisia), rigidity, stiffness and diminished spontaneity (akinesia), an expressionless face and possible muscle spasms. These side-effects are often short-lived and can usually be treated by anticholinergic drugs, the most common being procyclidine (*Kemadrin*) or phenadrine (*Disipal*). When the side-effects do not respond to drugs such as these it may be necessary to try a different anti-psychotic. Rigidity of the neck muscles, difficulty in turning the head, eyes fixed on the ceiling and difficulty in talking are, as a group, called dystomic reactions, and can be relieved immediately by drugs such as those above.

Some patients report a change in their sexual behaviour, usually in the form of decreased sexual desire. A few men may experience impotence (most likely if taking thioridazine [*Mellaril*]). This may be relieved by changing anti-psychotic drugs.

These side-effects are usually rated by doctors as 'not serious'. They may, however, cause great stress to sufferers and relatives. Reactions of sufferers to side-effects will vary. A little tremor may be tolerated or seen as 'nothing much' compared to the schizophrenic symptoms, but this same tremor may cause distress to the relative who has to watch it all day. For some sufferers decreased sexual desire may not be experienced as a problem since they are withdrawn and apathetic as part of the schizophrenia, but this may be experienced as a major problem by the sufferer's spouse. Other sufferers may experience the stiffness, rigidity or restlessness as greater problems than the doctor perceives them to be.

A side-effect that is more potentially serious is that increased photosensitivity may develop, when the person becomes very sensitive to the sun and will burn more easily. This is most likely with chlorpromazine (*Largactil*). This can be best controlled by using a strong sunscreen, wearing wide-brimmed hats and 'cover up' clothes and, where possible, staying in the shade. Another more serious side-effect, most common with chlorpromazine (*Largactil*) and fluphenazine (*Modecate*, etc.) and also trifluoperazine (*Stelazine*), is fainting when the person stands up after lying down. Weight gain may occur, and where this is in large amounts it should be seen as a major problem (even if the sufferer is not very upset by it). Although anti-psychotic drugs can cause weight gain in some people this may be aggravated by the inactivity of many chronic schizophrenic sufferers and indeed, caused by it in many cases. In any of these situations it might be necessary to transfer the person to another type of drug or take them off drugs altogether, at least for a period.

The last group of side-effects to concern us is known as tardive dyskinesia, which literally means late-appearing, disjointed movements. The movements which occur are involuntary (that is, not under the conscious control of the individual), principally connected with the mouth and tongue. For example, the person will make chewing or sucking movements, roll his tongue, smack his lips, blow out his cheeks or push them out with his tongue, make side to side movements of the chin and grimace. Sometimes these movements are also accompanied by jerky, disjointed movements of the arms or legs and, very occasionally, the whole body. This syndrome usually, but not always, develops in older people who have been on medication for quite some time. Although it usually begins whilst the patient is on drugs, in some rare instances it may not begin until medication has ceased.

In most instances these symptoms decrease and disappear when the drugs are stopped, but in some cases they persist. There is, at present, no effective treatment. For this reason the lowest dose of anti-psychotic medication which is effective should be used. Professionals, sufferers and relatives should be alert to symptoms, and the costs and benefits of neuroleptic drugs discussed clearly and calmly.

When to stop taking drugs

When acute symptoms are relieved then drugs should be reduced to a maintenance level, but whether they should be discontinued or not is a difficult decision to make. Some people have a return of acute symptoms when they stop drugs, others do not, and some find that residual problems are the same whether they are on drugs or not. This is an issue which should be openly discussed with your psychiatrist. Over the years you will possibly come to recognize the onset of a relapse and may begin extra medication quickly; you may even be able to prevent its worst excesses. Sadly, however, it is often when you feel most well and unwilling to take medication that you need it the most. If you have a psychiatrist whom you can trust, and who knows you well, your best bet is to be guided by him. Other factors, including the social environment of the patient, need to be taken into account in maintenance therapy and these will be discussed later.

When summing up the use of neuroleptic drugs in schizophrenia it may be as well to mention that studies have shown, overall, that about two-thirds of schizophrenic patients show a significant improvement on neuroleptics, and only one-tenth show no improvement at all.

Having previously said that drugs were only part of the answer, albeit the most important part in controlling acute symptoms, we now turn to the other forms of treatment which may be appropriate.

Psychotherapy

Psychotherapy is a fairly loose term and much depends on what is meant by it. Most people think immediately of Freud and psychoanalysis, but from the outset Freud said that psychoanalysis had nothing to offer the schizophrenic individual. In fact, none of the psychotherapies which aim to give the patient insight into the underlying, unconscious processes of the mind have any positive effect in treating schizophrenia and, indeed, may worsen the condition.

What may be termed 'supportive psychotherapy', however, may prove beneficial. What is most important here is a long-term, one-to-one relationship in which support and practical help and advice are given in helping the patient come to terms with his present situation. Support of this kind should be used in addition to drug therapy in most instances.

Psychotherapy may take place in a group situation rather than on an individual basis but, again, in its traditional, insight-oriented forms has nothing to offer the schizophrenic patient.

The Social Therapies

Again, there is no one simple definition of social therapy. It may include elements of supportive psychotherapy as well as more active, educational techniques. Although not helping acute symptoms it may help to prevent relapse and is particularly important in the rehabilitation of long-term chronic schizophrenic patients. Dealing with the problems of work, getting on with people, and day-to-day living may all come under the guise of social therapy.

Many of these learning activities will take place in a group situation as the patient comes to terms with the difficulties of living in the real world. Emphasis will often be given to involving the patient in various forms of activity to counteract social withdrawal and apathy, and the patient may be encouraged to take part in other therapies, such as occupational or industrial therapy.

Behaviour Therapy

Behaviour therapy is a set of techniques which may be used to help an individual learn new behaviour or to deal with problems. It concentrates on both the circumstances in which the behaviour occurs and the consequences of the behaviour. Again, it has little to offer the patient suffering acute symptoms, but is mainly useful in problems of withdrawal, apathy and the general rehabilitation of the chronic patient. The techniques may be used under the general guise of social therapies. Of special importance for some patients may be social skills training, to help them overcome some of their difficulties in relating to other people.

Industrial Therapy

The patient may be encouraged to take part in industrial therapy either within the hospital or at a special unit. The aims are broadly to develop the patient's confidence in a work situation and get him used to the discipline of a work routine. Units not attached to hospitals most closely approximate the work situation.

Family Therapy and the Family in Therapy

Few families are ever involved in full-scale family therapy and not many more are involved in the therapeutic process at all. This whole area will be discussed in Part Two. One new type of 'therapy' is one in which the relatives are being involved in education.

Education

The aim of this is to teach both patients and relatives about schizophrenia and, hopefully, how to deal with it. Although this may occur on an individual basis, it is more likely to be in group sessions involving both teaching sessions and discussions.

Rehabilitation

This is a general term used to cover a group of therapies and techniques designed to enable the patient to take his place in society. It will probably involve behavioural techniques, occupational therapy, groups of various kinds, social skills training, and training in everyday activities. Many hospitals have a separate rehabilitation unit in which long-stay patients live before being discharged, and where they are responsible for shopping, cooking, cleaning, washing and the like.

Vocational and educational testing may also play a part, as well as preliminary training in job skills, to enable the individual to compete in the job market.

Other Facilities

Day care facilities exist outside the hospital system and a patient may be referred to one of these. They incorporate various types of occupational therapy and some group work. Most also have some light industrial work for part of the day, such as packing, making boxes and and so on. Attendance and time-keeping are expected to be good.

Some areas have industrial rehabilitation units (IRU) which provide sheltered work, either as a training ground for the patient or on a more permanent basis. Attendance and time-keeping are expected to be the same as for someone at work.

Various forms of sheltered housing or group homes may be available, run by the hospital, local authority or a charity. These can provide either a stepping stone between the hospital and independence or a return to the family, or a more permanent living arrangement for those unable to manage on their own.

Self-Help Groups

These groups may prove invaluable for both patients and relatives, especially those who are receiving little help from elsewhere. Groups usually provide supportive relationships, a wealth of knowledge and practical experience and, perhaps most important of all, a place to air fears and worries in the knowledge that you will be understood by people with similar problems.

Past Therapies

Everyone has heard of some of the terrible treatments, in some instances almost resembling torture, that schizophrenic patients have been subjected to in the past. (In some instances the not-so-distant past.) The therapy which haunts people the most is electro-convulsive therapy (ECT, electrical treatment or 'shock' treatment). It is easy to find people who have had it in the past, or portrayals of it in the media which are negative, all of which add to its mystique and its frightening qualities. It is a controversial area, but it can be very useful for some patients, namely people who are severely depressed, especially if they are not responding to drugs. Nowadays it is only very rarely used for schizophrenic patients, and then usually only as a last resort for people who do not respond to drugs, who are severely disturbed and may be suicidal.

Treatment methods such as the insulin coma, binding the patient in wet sheets, strapping them to the bed or into a tub of cold water simply do not happen any more. A number of otherwise useful books about what it is like to be schizophrenic are now outdated on these points and any account of schizophrenia and its treatment should be read with reference to the *date* when things happened. Yes, it might be terrible, but this happened in the past and it should not stop you from having treatment in the *present* which is both more effective and more humane.

PART II
MANAGING SCHIZOPHRENIA
AT HOME

6.

THE PROBLEM IN THE FAMILY — SCHIZOPHRENIA AT HOME

This chapter, by its very title, makes one basic assumption and that is that having a schizophrenic patient living at home with the family is 'a problem'. In some instances this might not be true; having overcome the acute episode the individual may function well, may be able to return to his job and his social life with little difficulty. But, sadly, for many patients this is not the case.

The problems facing the family are many and varied. This chapter sets out the general orientation to problems and discusses some areas which affect everyone to a greater or lesser extent. Specific problems are discussed in more detail in the following chapters.

Whose Problem Is It?

The person who returns home from the hospital (or comes out of the acute episode) is not quite the same as they were before. Even if the worst of the bizarre behaviour has disappeared the person may now be withdrawn or isolated, hard to talk to and unwilling to do anything; at times he may appear sullen or moody, antisocial or hostile and at times downright bloody-minded. He may have no job to go to and may have lost contact with all, or at least most, of his friends. Those that are left quickly lose interest in the face of repeated hostility, rejection or apathy.

The family has to deal with this. With the best will in the world the person has become a 'problem'. But this is not the full extent of the difficulty. The patient himself has to live with the changes that have happened to him, often with the additional burden of being unable to find work, or work which is suitable, and often of a type not previously considered. He has to live with his family and friends and living in the same environment as before the attack may prove an intolerable strain. So living in the family is 'a problem' for the patient as well.

This is an important point for both parties to remember. Neither has chosen this course of events, it is something that has happened to them, and in virtually every case they would rather it had not. Every issue has two sides to it and whilst it may not be always possible to even remember that there *is* another side, let alone appreciate it, this is crucial to both dealing with that issue and developing a harmonious lifestyle. Both parties have difficulties in coming to terms with the situation, both parties view things differently, and this means that what each sees as 'a problem' will be different.

Problem . . . What Problem?

A common occurrence is that the sufferer, returning from hospital and not having a job to go to (or with the recommendation not to go back to work yet) and nothing much to do all day, spends most of the morning in bed. You, as his mother or father, view this as a problem, but you, the sufferer do not see anything wrong in it. Which of you is right? Is this a problem?

You may go to arbitration and ask your doctor or community nurse for their opinion. The majority will probably side with the parents. Why? They themselves get up early to go to work, they are conditioned to the idea that it is 'normal' to get up early and, wanting what is best for the sufferer, that is, wanting them to be 'normal', they insist on 'normal' behaviour. In some cases this might be the most sensible course of action, but is it in every case? Is it in this case?

Let us consider the situation further. Firstly, what is normal in these circumstances? If *you* had nowhere to go and nothing much to do would you be up early? Do you lie in at weekends? Or when you are on holiday? Would you get up early as you do during the week if it was not for work? Suppose you lived next door to your work and had no travelling, would you still get up at the same time or would you compensate by staying in bed longer? Furthermore, what is early? Seven o'clock? Eight o'clock? Nine o'clock? The time we get up and consider 'normal' for getting up is a well-conditioned habit of long-standing and we rarely question it; but if your lifestyle altered dramatically so would many of your habits. If this were aggravated by no real interest in, or motivation to do, anything, would you not choose to lie in bed most of the morning? Add to this several other considerations. It is warm and comfortable. There is little sense of time, so it appears to pass quickly. It is safe; it is private. No one disturbs you (apart maybe from yelling at you to get up, which can be easily blocked out).

This, then, is the sufferer's point of view. Or at least the most easily recognizable part of it; and not all of it is so odd either. Try several comparisons. For example, if the sufferer is fairly young, compare him with other people of his age. Do their mothers have problems getting them out of bed at weekends or during the holidays? What about unemployed people you may know — what time do they get up? If money is a problem remember the large number of elderly people, or those on low incomes, who admit to going to bed early, or staying in bed late, to save on heating. The picture begins to make more sense but, of course, this is not the whole picture. There may be adverse consequences. If the habit becomes so ingrained, or the lack of motivation so severe, that the sufferer simply *cannot* get up when it is necessary (e.g., to go to work, to go to a day centre, to attend hospital appointments) then it *is* a problem.

If the patient spends so much time in bed that he cannot sleep properly, then it *is* a problem. I have seen patients complain to doctors of being unable to sleep and receiving sleeping pills with no check on how long they were trying to sleep. Some were attempting to 'sleep' or at least stay in bed for sixteen to eighteen hours a day! Here the problem is not being able to sleep, but staying in bed and trying to sleep *too long*. By giving sleeping pills the doctor legitimized the wrong problem. If the sufferer expects to be given meals in bed and to have someone running around after him then it *is* a problem. The way this problem might best be tackled is outlined in Chapter 10.

There may be cases where these sets of considerations are not appropriate. Someone who chooses to lie in bed day after day and never gets up should be referred back to the psychiatrist. So should anyone who refuses to get up for meals and would rather miss them than get up.

Not only is the same behaviour described differently by sufferers and their relatives, but they may focus their attention on very different areas. A survey I carried out with the members of the National Schizophrenia Fellowship in Scotland indicated that the problems in the forefront of patients' and relatives' minds varies dramatically. In both groups there was wide variation, with some agreement on the sufferers' social problems and isolation, but the relatives tended to be unaware of the additional problems the sufferers cited, such as poor concentration, residual symptoms and so forth. Relatives also detailed the problems *they* had in dealing with the sufferer, and the effect of the illness on their life, things which did not seem to occur to the sufferer. In some instances there is little or no communication in this area, and neither side is aware of the difficulties of the other. This is not always easily dealt with, but simply rectifying the lack of communication might alleviate some difficulties.

So we begin to have a system for looking at 'a problem' and deciding whether it really is one or not.

1. Who thinks it is a problem? Why?
2. Who does not think it is a problem? Why?
3. Are there benefits from the behaviour?
4. Are there adverse consequences from the behaviour?
5. Do these affect whether it is described as a problem?
6. Can any of the benefits be changed and attached to more appropriate behaviour?

Different Families Have Different Problems

Having established the fact that sufferers and relatives may see issues differently, and thus call different behaviours problems, we turn to consider the differences between families. What is seen as a problem depends not just on the behaviour itself, but on its context, that is, the whole set of circumstances surrounding it, including the type of family. Families where the sufferer is the child (albeit an adult child) may see things very differently from families where the sufferer is a spouse or even a parent.

Research has shown that the type of family a patient returns to affects behaviour and relapse rate. We will come on to some important work in this area in the next chapter, but for now it is enough to note that parental families (i.e., where an adult child returns to live with his parents) tolerate more 'ill' behaviour than do marital families. The reasons for this might have a number of roots, but probably owe much to the different type of relationship and expectancies of the families. Parents, particularly mothers, who have spent years caring for their children may find it easier to tolerate 'childish' or dependent behaviour than does a wife, who expects her husband to share adult responsibilities with her. A wife may resent her husband stepping into the role of a child, especially if she already has young children to deal with, and she may find this additional burden, as well as running the family, too much to cope with. The sufferer in this position may also have been, or was expected to be, the principal breadwinner and the family may suffer financial difficulty if he is out of work for prolonged periods of time, or if he has to return to a less well paid job. At the same time, the marital family, in tolerating ill behaviour less well and expecting more of the sufferer, may encourage the individual to pick up the reins of his old life more quickly and more effectively and may thus pull him out of the damaging secondary symptoms. On the other hand, in some cases these stresses may prove too much for the person and may precipitate him into another relapse.

Where there are children in a family, be they the children of the sufferer, or his younger brothers and sisters, there will be other sorts of problems: how to explain the situation to them, how to help them deal with it, and their worries concerning it.

Most sufferers returning to their family are returning to a parental family, but even here there is opportunity for great diversity in perceived problems. Families differ in their ability to tolerate bizarre behaviour. Some will allow the patient to talk about his strange beliefs with no comment and little interest, others will feel uneasy and shun the person at such times, still others will be unable to let the matter rest until they have convinced the person he is wrong and therefore will engage in endless arguments, and all of this may depend on who else is about. Strange behaviour may not bother you unduly unless someone else is there (a friend or more distant relative), or you are in a public place, when you may become less able to tolerate it, becoming uneasy or embarrassed.

Some families who seem to be able to deal with remarkable amounts of strange behaviour in the sufferer, e.g. talking to or about people they cannot see, or expressing odd ideas may, however, find it difficult to cope with other aspects of behaviour; this may include poor hygiene, or social withdrawal, or the person never volunteering to do any chores, or sitting silently for hours on end, or whatever. The reason I stress this point is to emphasize that even if you have a similar situation to another family, the way you view it will be different and it is this view that needs to be conveyed to the professionals with whom you are dealing. They can only work from what they see or think is important, or most

distressing, or what experience with other families has shown
them to be problem areas. If your circumstances are different,
or other things worry you, you should be able to mention this
and talk it over. It may be that it is something they have not
considered, or that nothing can be done or, in the patient's best
interest, they may disagree with you. Nevertheless, it is important
for both sides to feel free to discuss these issues.

In the previously-mentioned survey the range of problems to
which the relatives gave priority was very wide. Many such
problems will need to be experienced firsthand for their true
impact to be felt, others are daily irritating habits which wear away
at a person's patience and compassion. The professional does
not live with the patient — you do and it is important to put *your*
point of view across. Dealing with professionals is not always easy
and is covered in Chapter 11. Education is especially important
here. Knowing about the illness means that you can appreciate
the sufferer's position more and deal more clearly and
competently with what the psychiatrist says. It also means that
you can be more realistic in your goals and expectations.

Objective and Subjective Burdens

From research that was started in the 1960s the burden which
falls on the family, a name for the total amount of problems they
have to deal with, has been divided into two parts. The 'objective
burden' has to do with the part that everybody can see, can
measure and can understand is a burden. It includes all the physical
and material burdens placed on the family, burdens of time, energy
and resources. It includes having to give up time to spend with
the person because he cannot be left on his own, the energy
needed to care for someone who cannot manage on his own,
the money lost by the sufferer not working and, possibly,
someone having to give up work to stay at home with him.

The subjective burden has to do with the way this affects you,
the stress you feel, your ability to cope with the strains that having
the sufferer to live with you causes. Families, and indeed individual
members of families, cope with this differently. To an outsider
one family may seem to have more of a burden than another,
in objective terms, and yet can cope better. Reasons for this are
hard to find and are certainly not universal. Maybe they are just
more tolerant, or easy-going, or they have lower expectations,
or they are in agreement and share the burden. This latter point

might be particularly important. It is rare for a family to agree on this issue. Whilst one parent may recognize the illness, the other may label the sufferer lazy or stupid or uncaring and refuse to have anything much to do with him. One parent, or sibling or a child, may find the whole idea of mental illness confusing and frightening. They may see it as a stigma on the family and on *them* and try to hide from the knowledge and hide the truth from others outside the family.

In these cases, the burden of care will fall unequally on the family members who are left. Even in the cases of reasonable agreement the main burden of care usually falls on the mother. It is she who has to do the extra work, extra cooking, cleaning and washing. It is usually she who is left to urge the patient to wash, to take his medication, to find something to do. If anyone has to give up a job to stay at home, it is the mother whose job goes. Even if she was not working, she is the person who is at home with the sufferer all day, every day, week after week, frequently year after year with no respite. No matter how much she loves her child this is a tremendous burden to bear, and one which other family members should recognize and try to lessen. I know of families where the father will tell you that the sufferer is coming on 'just fine', where he is off drugs 'because he does not like them' and is behaving bizarrely 'but we think it is better for him' and who says that, all things considered, he is 'fairly happy with the situation'. But in these same families the mother is constantly tired, anxious and depressed, she takes tranquillizers and sleeping tablets, but still sleeps and eats poorly, she looks older than her years and seems to find little in life to enjoy, rarely getting out of the house for anything other than shopping. These are the people who, together with the sufferer, carry the full burden of schizophrenia.

Stress
Stress is often cited as one of the triggering effects of schizophrenia, and also an effect of schizophrenia on the family. What exactly is meant by this and what constitutes stress in these conditions? These are complex questions to answer and examples will be given in the chapters on relatives' and sufferers' problems.

Basically though, something can be called a stressor (that is, something which causes stress in the individual) when the individual cannot cope with it in an adaptive (that is, healthy) fashion. The individual copes in a maladaptive or unhealthy way, whether this is having a schizophrenic breakdown or becoming tense or anxious. It seems that the person who becomes schizophrenic is particularly sensitive to stressors in the environment and can tolerate these less well than a non-schizophrenic individual. This is not to say that given enough stress anyone will become schizophrenic — that is not so. The person who becomes schizophrenic is predisposed to this, the stress triggers it.

What type of stressor and how much stress causes a relapse are important questions when managing schizophrenia on a day-to-day basis. The answers tend to be individual and need careful monitoring by both the schizophrenic sufferer and his family.

Most people can recognize that too much stress is a bad thing, but the converse is also true. Too little stimulation can also be a problem for the schizophrenic sufferer. Just as too much stress may cause the person to withdraw, both from social interaction and from general activities, in an attempt to protect himself, so, once in this withdrawn state, he finds it increasingly hard to do anything, to find any motivation or interest in activities which are either necessary or which he previously enjoyed. Without sufficient appropriate stimulation the withdrawal will become deeper and harder for the person to come out of. As in other areas a balance between too much and too little stimulation is necessary. What this means for each sufferer is different and can only be worked out by a mixture of trial and error and by drawing on the experience of others, be they professionals, sufferers or relatives.

Two areas are particularly important and have wide applicability. One is the effect of life events, as previously mentioned. The second is the effect of the family itself on the sufferer, and in particular the stressful effects of certain sorts of communication within the family. We turn to look at this problem and possible solutions in more detail now.

7.

COMMUNICATION IN THE FAMILY

The Emotional Involvement of the Family

How the family comes to terms with the knowledge that one of their members has schizophrenia and then how it deals with that person will vary enormously. Some families, or family members, will become critical and hostile, objecting to the sufferer and everything he does and says. Others may go to the opposite extreme and be especially caring and protective, making tremendous allowances for the fact that the person is ill and 'cannot help what he is doing'; they urge the sufferer to 'concentrate on getting well' whilst they take over the responsibilities of the sufferer to himself and others, much as though he were a child. Some families somehow manage to steer a middle course, treating the sufferer much the same as everyone else.

Research carried out in London at the Institute of Psychiatry has been concerned with this very point — the emotional involvement of the family with the patient. They are particularly concerned about families with high expressed emotion and the effect that this has on the patient. In most instances, high expressed emotion means emotion which would be seen as negative by anybody observing it, such as hostile, critical and generally negative comments. But another form that high expressed emotion takes is that of over-protectiveness, where the family or one family member tries to protect the sufferer from the stresses of everyday living in a very over-concerned way. One important finding in this research is to show that both types of high expressed emotion have negative outcomes for the sufferer. When this type of communication is combined with high face to face contact in the family (the researchers defined this as over thirty-five hours per week) then the negative effects are particularly powerful, and even maintenance drug therapy may not be enough to prevent relapse.

The patients who do the best are in families which, to some, might seem indifferent, bordering on the uncaring. It is not that they are uninvolved or indifferent; but they are able to express a natural degree of warmth and caring without being over-protective or smothering, coupled with a detachment and matter-of-factness about the patient's bizarre or anti-social ideas or behaviour which in no way becomes critical or hostile. Such remarkable families are to be admired and emulated, since they seem to have found one of the main keys to maintaining the sufferer's fragile mental stability.

However, to talk of reducing the high emotional involvement of families, which the sufferer experiences as stressful and the family as either their right to complain or to express caring, is one thing, and to achieve this is a very different matter. The latter is often a hard, uphill struggle. Wherever possible try to discuss this with a sympathetic and knowledgeable professional — one who knows the literature in this area. This will be particularly important if you are not sure if you fall into one or other of these categories yourself. Over-protectiveness in particular is hard to see in ourselves, we rationalize it as a practical and realistic expression of our concern — we may need a more objective outsider to point out how our smothering behaviour stifles initiative and responsibility.

In some instances, where lowering emotional involvement is difficult, or where it is so high and widespread, an adjunct or alternative may be for the sufferer to spend less time with the family. This may range from him moving out completely to live in a hostel or sheltered accommodation of some kind, to spending a few hours a day at some sort of day centre or social club.

Reducing the Expression of Emotional Involvement
Even if it is not possible for your feelings to undergo a radical change, or at least not quickly, it is possible to learn to communicate with the sufferer in a way which is less stressful to him. Even if your prime concern is to reduce the negative effects of the sufferer on the family this is probably best done by helping the sufferer to maintain some sort of equilibrium and avoiding relapse as far as possible.

1. Good times, bad times

At the outset it must be acknowledged that there will be good times and bad times. As far as possible maximize the good times, making the most of the opportunities they present. These are the times when it is possible to build some sort of relationship with the sufferer, when he may actively seek out family members and try to establish rapport with them. It is during this time that a trusting relationship can be established which will not only help carry you through bad times, but which sometimes may be used to positive advantage during them. Use them to learn.

a) *Discuss bad times*

If possible, during the good times try to get the sufferer to describe some of the things that happen to him when he is ill (without putting undue stress on him) and what he thinks could help most at these times, or what he would like you to do. Many sufferers are much more aware of what is going on around them, what people are doing and saying, than they appear to be during periods of seeming total loss of contact with reality. Thus the sufferer may be able to describe why he rejected offers of help, or took objection to things which were done or said. In the light of this, his disordered thinking at the time his behaviour may then begin to make more sense.

If he can say, 'The reason I threw the apple you offered me back at you was because I could see snakes coming out of it/I thought you were trying to poison me/I thought you were indicating you knew I had sinned and were trying to make me confess', then the feeling of personal rejection which the relative experienced can be discharged. Or the sufferer may express feelings such as, 'I felt very frightened at the time and although I was telling you to leave me alone I felt much safer when you stayed'. These are particularly important pieces of information to have as they tell you how to behave during the next 'bad times'.

b) *No recriminations*

The good times should be used in a positive way, not to talk over how bad things have been for the family, how much he hurt, upset, embarrassed or worried you. If you can explain some of your behaviour, whilst discussing how he felt in the bad times, this may clear up some misunderstandings. Even if all you can explain is 'I didn't know how best to help, and since I only seemed to be upsetting you, I thought it best to leave. I was not rejecting you,' this gives the basis for discussion, in a way that statements such as, 'If you knew how much your behaviour upset your mother you wouldn't do it', 'After all I have done for you to have you shout at me like that . . .' 'How any son of mine could . . .' etc., do not.

c) Participation in family events
During good times try to include the sufferer in family activities in the way you would any other family member, neither pressing him to do something he clearly does not want to, but encouraging him wherever and whenever there is a glimmer of positive response or enthusiasm to a suggestion. Loss of confidence in self is characteristic of many recovering schizophrenics and they need all the support you can give them. In private this can be open and overt: 'Come on John, I know you can do it, and we will be there to help'; but in public the displays of support should be more subtle and not open for all to see and hear, unless the situation makes it acceptable. For example, it might be appropriate to shout support, encouragement and even advice to someone taking part in a sporting event, but not if the situation is that of a visit to relatives.

2. Bizarre ideas
Most of the sufferer's strange and bizarre ideas or behaviour will spring from delusions and hallucinations. These will usually be most pronounced during periods of breakdown, but some of the odd ideas may linger on into the sufferer's well periods. The basic rule is not to argue. It does not matter how silly and irrational the idea, or how rational or practical your arguments, you will not dislodge the idea and are only encouraging the sufferer to dwell on, and talk about, his obsession. If, at some stage, you find yourself drawn into a discussion about his ideas or hallucinations, through trying to understand what he is saying or doing, you should always make it clear that you do not agree, that you accept that he believes what he is saying and that you are not going to argue the point. It is usually counterproductive to try to humour the sufferer by pretending to agree, since he will often sense that it is a pretence and become suspicious of you and your motives, or even hostile.

If the sufferer persists in his strange beliefs, and in talking about them in public, in some instances it is possible to confine what he says to a straightforward statement which at face value makes sense. For example, one sufferer told everyone he had food poisoning (his delusion). His story only became strange if you asked him how long he had been ill (seven years) or how he knew he had food poisoning ('by the silver cloud hovering over my head'). But on a day-to-day basis with people he did not know, but came into contact with briefly, and with whom he wanted to talk, it served as a reasonable explanation and few followed it up.

As well as not arguing with ideas which stem from delusions, it is best not to try too hard to persuade a person from engaging in bizarre behaviour once it has started (unless it is violent and actively dangerous towards something or someone). If he talks to himself or to people who are not there, giggles or laughs to himself, or stares fixedly into space, remember that to him his behaviour makes sense — he is simply seeing reality differently from you. It may be possible to distract his attention, particularly if you can spot this behaviour in its early stages. Trying to engage the patient in conversation probably will not work, since this is not enough to compete with what is happening inside his head. Physical activity (it need only be fairly minor) and the need to pay visual attention are important. Sometimes, where you have to compete with other voices, listening as well may help, but on its own it rarely drowns out other things. If this can be combined with co-operating with you on a task this may be even better. These events may range from helping with chores, to doing something in the garden, or engaging in some hobby. It helps if it is something the person enjoys, or at least does not actively dislike or resent. In such a case this strategy may be of no use at all.

Sometimes it is the emotion which accompanies the strange beliefs that causes the problem. If the sufferer is calm, or even enjoys his delusions and hallucinations, one might argue that we should not try to prevent him enjoying them. On the other hand, if he is obviously upset, worried or distressed by the topic then this is an entirely different situation. Not only is there the observable suffering, but the possibility that he might act on these beliefs. Again, one should not argue since it is unlikely to do any good. The first thing to check is the sufferer's medication, since it is possible that he has stopped taking it or that the amount has been changed.

Another reason for the increase in strange ideas, or talking about them may be because the sufferer is more stressed than usual. The increase in delusional ideas may then be in response to the stress, or may be a way of dealing with the stress. These sorts of stress may be connected with an ongoing situation or to some particular event that has happened. The reaction to a stressful life event may not be immediate, but may take several weeks to show itself. If the problem of talking about delusions persists, particularly if it is accompanied by signs of distress, then it should always be reported to the doctor, with the patient's knowledge even if not his permission. Included with this should be any information that might be relevant, e.g. to do with medication or new stresses in the sufferer's life.

Another aspect of bizarre ideas involves the interpretation that the sufferer puts on things which other people do or say. He may misunderstand remarks made by friends or other family members and twist them into meaning something entirely different and possibly of sinister intent. Usually the sufferer will have distorted what has been said and may relate it to paranoid delusions or simply to the fact that he has been ill. The everyday greeting 'How are you?' may be seen to have a special reference to the sufferer, referring to the fact that he has been ill and is possibly becoming ill again. Sometimes such distortions can be cleared up quickly, at other times not. Again you should not argue with the patient but state calmly, clearly and rationally what you meant and leave it at that. Discussion of 'what was *really* meant' should be avoided.

On some occasions, however, the sufferer's interpretation may be correct. Some schizophrenics are especially sensitive to atmosphere and they may pick up negative feelings which you are either unaware of or trying to hide. This means that not only should you try to control your more extreme feelings when dealing with the sufferer, but also that they should find a release somewhere, so that they are not constantly bottled up, ready to break loose at the wrong moment. It is possible, in time, to learn to say that something the sufferer has done has either upset or displeased you, in a rational way, without overcharging the situation with emotion which neither of you may be able to handle.

3. Keep coming back
Particularly through the bad times relatives may be on the receiving end of a lot of hostility or rejection from the sufferer.

In some instances it may be not be so open and blatant as this, but may take the form of a slow and silent withdrawal from everyone and everything. Always bear in mind that this rejection springs from the illness itself. It is true that there might be some bizarre relationships within families which make the rejection not only real, but sensible and self-protective, but this is not generally the case.

If, as I suggested earlier, this can be talked through when the patient is well (with no recrimination or blame) then it will be easier to understand and deal with when it happens again. The sufferer may say that on some occasions when he is ill he really does mean it when he says 'Go away' because it is too painful or too stressful to have people he cares about see him in that state, or the emotions engendered are too much to deal with, or even that *at that moment* he truly believes something bad about you. Especially with the latter it is vital to remember that at that time he is ill and not in control of his thoughts. When he is well again he knows it to be untrue but also, that if he is ill again, *he may well believe it again*.

When the patient is ill treat him as positively as you can, take advice from involved professionals about how much contact you should have and whether your visits to the hospital upset him. If the doctor suggests that you do not visit for a while remember that his first concern is for his patient, in this case the sufferer, and if his instructions cause you some distress this is of secondary concern to him.

When the patient is going through a good period do not let resentments from the bad times spill over and prevent you doing things now. Even if he rejected you then he may want the opportunity to be with you, and to do things with you now. Or if you invite him to do something and he does not want to, do not give up, try another time, or try something different. A thick skin is an important requirement when dealing with someone with schizophrenia, and even if your feelings are hurt, and you cry in private, you must still keep coming back and offering support and friendship. The next time *may* be the time the sufferer can accept it.

Telling Friends and Relatives

One difficult area seems to be not only how to tell friends and other family members what the problem is, but also how much to tell them and in some instances who to tell.

To start with the last point first, it is going to be obvious to anyone living in, or having close contact with, the family, that there is a problem and that something strange is happening; therefore they should be told what the problem is, details of what is happening and, where appropriate, details of treatment and future plans. Whether you choose to tell all relatives and friends about the problem is largely up to you but, wherever possible, tell the truth. It would be inappropriate to go into details with everyone, but if you lie and deny the problem, or deny that the sufferer is having treatment/attending the hospital/on drugs/ or anything else, then this is an additional strain. You have to remember who knows what, what stories you have concocted to explain the sufferer's absence, either from home for periods or from a family event, and so on. Often the more you try to hide, the more suspicious people will become and they will try to find out what you are hiding. When they do find out they may be hurt or angry that you did not trust them enough to tell them the truth, or may assume that you are ashamed and embarrassed by the sufferer's illness. The sufferer himself may feel the latter if you try too strenuously to hide the truth.

This does not mean that you need to tell everyone everything. Using the word schizophrenia is difficult for many people: it conjures up so many frightening visions. If you are going to tell anyone the diagnosis, it is as well to have a brief speech ready and then explain what schizophrenia is, to explain that it is *not* 'Jekyll and Hyde', that the patient *is not* violent. If you find this too difficult, leaflets produced by the National Schizophrenia Fellowship, MIND or even a couple of pages copied out of a book might be useful. Allow people to ask questions, and answer as honestly as you can. The more people know about schizophrenia and the more it is talked about, the less frightening the word will become.

You may feel, however, that you do not want to be that much of a pioneer, and that you do not want everyone to know the diagnosis. That also is your choice, and the sufferer's. Much depends on how much he wants others to be told. Neighbours and acquaintances may need to be told little more than that there is a problem, and that the sufferer is having treatment or is under the care of the hospital. The terms 'nervous breakdown' and 'mental breakdown' do not have any diagnostic significance and can be used to cover a multitude of problems and conditions, and so can 'emotional problems' and 'psychological problems'.

Simply because someone is ill does not give everyone else the right to know everything about them, so never say more than the sufferer wants you to say (with the possible exception of the people you live with — but explain what you are saying and why, to the sufferer) or what you want the other person to know. Sometimes people's curiosity about illness, particularly mental illness, gets a little out of hand. Remember you do not have to have them intruding into your family's privacy and you can refuse to answer.

When you tell people of the problem, try to do so in a straight-forward and matter-of-fact way. It sometimes helps people to understand if the facts are separated from your fears and anxieties about the problem. These can then be discussed separately and in their own right, without long detours into explaining facts that the other person needs to know to understand your feelings. One group in particular needs sensitive handling when discussing these matters and that is children.

Telling children
'Children' covers everyone from the very young to those in their teens, and they may be the children of the sufferer or siblings. The older the child the more likely he is to have been aware of the problem since the beginning, and he may have found his own life considerably affected by the sufferer.

As a basis children should be told that the sufferer is ill, that his odd ideas are real to him and that is why he might act strangely, that he cannot help his behaviour at times and that he will be difficult to deal with sometimes. Like everyone else children will respond differently. They should be encouraged to talk about their feelings towards the sufferer, his behaviour, the way he treats them and the effect this illness has on their life. If the child expresses resentment and hostility, and is old enough to understand a rational argument, you may want to try to present the sufferer's point of view and inability to control the situation; but you should not try to talk the child out of his feelings. They will be normal, natural and understandable and the child must have an opportunity to express them and receive support or help in dealing with them. Do not try to make the child deny these feelings, or to make him feel guilty for experiencing them.

Sometimes the child may find it easier to express these feelings to someone outside the immediate family, whether this is an aunt, a friend's parent or a teacher at school. If the child chooses to do this, acquaint the person with enough facts and details for them to be able to handle the situation successfully. If the child is experiencing severe problems in coming to terms with the situation, and especially if this interferes over a period of time with his behaviour either at home or at school, he may benefit from talking with a person experienced in these matters such as a social worker, child guidance counsellor or even a child psychologist.

When the child is being honest about his feelings, be honest about your own. If the sufferer has done something which has upset the whole family admit that you are upset too, e.g. 'I am cross with Daddy as well at the moment, but we'll get over it'. At other times, though, get the child to talk about what the sufferer does for him that he enjoys and get the child to tell him. Point out to the child positive aspects of the sufferer's behaviour to get the child to see them, e.g., 'It was nice of your brother to read to you, wasn't it?' The aim is to get the child to accept the sufferer as part of the family unit, as someone who has feelings which must be considered, who can do kind and positive things, but who can also do strange and antisocial things, and that it is acceptable to reject this latter behaviour.

Lastly, and most importantly, make sure that the children understand they are *always* to tell you *immediately* if the sufferer does anything that frightens them or which they think might be dangerous. If for some reason you are not around then they are to go to another responsible adult; give them examples, e.g. 'If I am not here, tell Auntie Mary next door'. In some instances taking immediate action to prevent the sufferer harming himself might be necessary, but always let the child talk through the event at some time and express his fears. If something the patient does which frightens the child persists, then the doctor should be informed and measures taken to deal with this behaviour.

Family Reactions

Not everyone will respond the same way — some will have patience, tolerance and understanding, others will not. Some will do a lot to be supportive and helpful, others will not. Some will become bitter and resentful, others will not. The effect of the sufferer on other members of the family can be enormous and this must be discussed.

Siblings may have their life severely disrupted. They may feel that they cannot bring friends home, their sleep and studies may be disturbed, and as a result they may feel justified resentment. This should be discussed as openly as possible, with the sufferer present, and the family should try to agree on solutions. Almost inevitably such solutions will be compromises but at least everyone will understand the other's position and will see that everything possible is being done to arrive at a solution. If even compromise solutions seem unattainable, and hostility and resentment to the sufferer becomes unmanageable, an outside person may be useful in helping the family to deal with the problem. This could be the patient's own doctor, a psychologist or social worker or family counsellor. If the sufferer's behaviour is causing problems in the marital relationship, because the parents cannot agree, then a marriage guidance counsellor may help in airing differences.

Sometimes one person will seem to understand the sufferer better than anyone else, or the sufferer will seek out a special person to talk to and confide in. This is not always the person who does the most for him and who bears the major burden. This can cause some resentment and jealousy, which is natural, but it is good that the sufferer has someone whom he thinks can help and support him. So many cannot reach out to anyone in this way at all, and this may be an important step forward.

8.

RELATIVES' PROBLEMS

When one member of a family has a severe, chronic illness, he is not the only one who suffers problems. The whole family is affected and not just as individuals, but as a unit. Broadly speaking, the problems and difficulties experienced can be categorized into three areas:

1. Dealing with the patient, his illness and symptoms, behaviour, emotions and problems and the effect that these have on the family.
2. Dealing with the effects of the relative's illness on yourself, your feelings about it and how you cope with the additional problems and burdens.
3. Dealing with the people from whom you should get help, whether as individual professionals, or as part of a bureaucracy or organization from which it is difficult to get what you need or want.

The major part of the second section of this book is concerned with the first set of problems. Chapter 11 deals with getting help and getting the best out of the agencies available. The present chapter looks at the responses and problems of the relatives.

How Do You Cope?
Families and individuals will have different ways of coping. In part this depends on the type of relative you are to the patient; mothers will feel differently to wives, and indeed to fathers. This in turn relates to the effect the illness, and consequent disruption, has on you and your life, the burden you have to carry. Part also depends on such individual features as personality, tolerance and ability to cope. Relatives can be broadly categorized as content, resigned or dissatisfied. Although simply knowing which category

you fall into is not in itself of particular importance, it may help you to crystallize some of your ideas about the difficulties you have, to put others in perspective and to aid in assessing your priorities. If you have always felt yourself to be fairly resigned to the problem, but in fact are dissatisfied in major ways, it is better for all concerned to have this out in the open and to face up to it, even if at the end of the day nothing can be done and resignation is the only choice.

Type of burden

The type of burden you carry as a relative is a crucial part of how you, as an individual, cope, although different people with the same burden may respond very differently, so research does not necessarily link type of burden with type of coping. Types of burden are discussed in Chapter 6. There is clearly some measure of overlap between type of burden, and professionals, relatives and sufferers have three different views on what is, or is not, a problem. How far a patient can take care of himself, for example, is a good case in point.

The professional *knows* that the sufferer *can* wash and dress himself, has seen him do so in hospital, and sees him at hospital appointments fairly clean and neatly dressed. On the other hand the relative *knows* that the sufferer *does not* get washed and dressed without a great deal of nagging, and that he needs some help in looking fairly tidy, e.g., tying ties, straightening clothes, being co-ordinated and, most important, wearing clean clothes. Washing and dressing is a daily battle. The sufferer's position may vary from not understanding what all the hassle is about, to saying he cannot, or will not comply, or that there is no point in dressing if he is not going anywhere.

There is also overlap in that the objective problems may be the cause of the subjective worries. If someone, usually a mother, has had to give up a job to stay at home with the sufferer, the problem is not just a financial one but includes a natural measure of resentment, loss of companionship and stimulation, and a narrowing of horizons which must be acknowledged and dealt with.

It is important to be both honest and clear with yourself, as well as the professionals, in terms of what you experience as burden. Often, it is not the 'big' things that cause the most distress and tension in the family, but the small, trivial things that happen day after day. This does not make them less real or less important and unless you are clear about what it is that causes the most rows or tension, and can tell the professional when asked, then any help which might be forthcoming will be directed at what the professional thinks is the problem, which might be something entirely different.

Dealing with Feelings

Guilt and blame

Many relatives experience feelings of guilt when a member of the family becomes seriously ill, even if only on the level of 'why them and not me?' When someone becomes psychiatrically ill the scope for guilt is even wider. Thoughts centre around worries such as, 'Where did we go wrong?' 'How did I treat him differently from his brothers and sisters?' 'Could I have prevented this?' 'Should I have done something about it earlier?' and 'Am I to blame?'

Not only parents will experience guilt feelings; spouses may also feel that in some way they may have contributed to the problem: 'He was OK until we were married', 'Maybe I am not the sort of husband she really wanted' 'Did I push him into getting married?' Even siblings or the children of the schizophrenic may not escape these feelings, and even very young children can feel that they have contributed to someone's breakdown, often simply through being naughty and not doing as they have been told. Siblings may worry that they have caused the illness by their jealousy of a brother or sister, or by childish taunts and wishes such as 'I wish you were dead'.

Firstly it is important to recognize that these guilt feelings exist, that they are fairly normal and natural but can become a major problem if they get out of hand. In part the guilt may spring from feelings of relief: relief that it *is not* you who are ill, relief that it has been diagnosed as an illness and you do not have to try to pretend any more; and even relief when someone is admitted into hospital and you get a break from the daily grind. If you, as well as the sufferer, are going to benefit from his hospital admission, then experiencing excessive guilt will do nothing for you. Saying that is easier than turning off the guilt, but it can be done. Discussing the problem with a sympathetic professional may help, especially if they can help you understand that the causes of schizophrenia lie, to a large part, within the biochemical structure of the individual. Even if stress in some form does play a part in the person developing schizophrenia, it is likely that the person is extra sensitive to everyday stresses, rather than always having more stress than other people.

Accept that whatever happened in the past is past, and even *if* (and it's a big if) something you may have done has contributed to the problem, then also be fair to yourself and acknowledge that you *did not* set out to cause the person harm, that you acted with the best of intentions, in the way that seemed best to you as a result of your upbringing and experiences. We are all the product of our families and our environment as our parents were of theirs. Looking to blame *one* person or one incident for causing something that is the result of so many influences is worse than looking for a needle in a haystack.

Sometimes, however, there are sufferers who have been subjected to very strange, upsetting or disturbing incidents, or their whole upbringing has been one which we would describe as abnormal. Again, this should be discussed where possible with a sympathetic professional and then, if not forgotten, not dwelt on. Many children experience at least one disturbing incident in their childhood without becoming ill, and there are people who have withstood a 'strange upbringing'. To become schizophrenic the biochemical possibility for becoming schizophrenic must be present.

What do you do about such feelings of blame? 'It's her father's fault, he never believed she was his', 'If his mother had not treated him like a sissy and protected him from everything', 'His brothers never let him play with them, always kept him out of their games' may be true statements as you see it, but may have little to do with why anyone develops schizophrenia. The past is the past; what matters now is the future and how you handle that.

Sometimes expressions of blame and guilt are a way of expressing all sorts of feelings which we may have and to which we cannot always put a name. You may try to bottle up worry and anxiety only to find it all spilling out in a tirade of blame aimed at someone else in the family. Frequently we see expressions of guilt as a sign of caring. The more upset someone is, the more worried and anxious he is, the more he blames himself for what has happened, the more he seems to demonstrate he cares. Whilst I am not saying that such people do not care, they probably do not care more than others who do not behave like this but take a more positive attitude, look to the future and what can be done, or generally maintain a more optimistic outlook. Some people seem naturally to be like this, but it is an attitude that can be learnt.

If you experience a lot of guilt feelings and the sorts of worries and anxieties that get you nowhere practically, ask yourself if you are not getting something out of them. Maybe they stop you feeling heartless for enjoying yourself when your child is ill, or show friends and relatives how much you still love the sufferer, or even what a martyr you are. Negative feelings, worries, anxieties, guilt and self-pity can become a habit. We can become so used to experiencing them that if we realize that, at a particular moment, we do not feel any of them we can then quickly talk ourselves into feeling them again. Resolve to try to reverse these feelings, so that when you become aware that you are indulging in a fit of self-pity you will stop saying the negative things to yourself and try to look positively and realistically to the future and what can be done. If nothing else you might choose to spend some of these times reading about schizophrenia and trying to learn more about the illness and its problems.

It is not that I am unsympathetic to the relatives' problems and feelings but the more you can do to help yourself, and deal with your own problems, the easier your life will be. This is better for the sufferer, which is ultimately better for you.

Embarrassment

Just as many relatives of schizophrenics experience feelings of guilt at some time, so too do many feel embarrassment and, again, such feelings may be to some extent normal, natural and understandable. They might, in turn, lead to further feelings of guilt.

Much of the embarrassment and shame stems from awareness of other people's perceptions of the problems and illness. Sometimes it is easier if other people know the person is ill, then there is an explanation for the strange behaviour and people may be more sympathetic to someone who is 'ill' rather than 'odd'. Schizophrenia is generally misunderstood and has a bad press and this does not help in people's understanding of the problems.

All types of relatives can experience feelings of embarrassment and will express them in slightly different ways, ranging from, 'Will people think he is like this as a result of something I have done?' to, 'People will think there must be something wrong with me to have married someone like this'. Adults might acknowledge such feelings, and be aware that other people regard the sufferer strangely, but this problem can often be more difficult for children and teenagers. Although some adults can be very insensitive and careless in what they say, most will keep their feelings about the sufferer's behaviour to themselves. Children, however, are more likely to be open and ruthlessly honest in what they say and may indulge in quite cruel teasing, either of the sufferer himself or his siblings or children. A consequence of this might be that the children gradually withdraw from others, choosing to play by themselves rather than come in for such teasing. They may stop inviting children round to the house if the sufferer's behaviour will embarrass them, and may then stop visiting their friends if they feel they cannot reciprocate. Other children may respond differently and get into fights with those who are rude about the sufferer. Such aggressive behaviour itself may lead to isolation and other types of problems at school.

Where this is happening it may be useful to explain the problem to the child's class teacher at school to see if something can be done there to ease the situation. Since people are often frightened by what they do not understand, and may deal with this by making fun of it, inviting one or two of the child's friends to tea with their parents may help. This should be done slowly and carefully so as not to put too much stress on the sufferer, and he should be allowed to escape from the situation if he so wishes, but if people can see that here is a quiet, shy, withdrawn person who is not going to harm anyone, some of *their* anxieties and embarrassment about mixing may disappear.

Of course, the sufferer's behaviour may well be embarrassing and antisocial and others may quite reasonably be put off by it. In this case it might be acceptable to exclude the sufferer from some things. Families do not always do everything together and there is no reason why the sufferer must always be included in everything. If the sufferer is to be excluded from something because of antisocial behaviour, tell him so, rather than let him think he is being rejected as a person. 'Mary must have friends in to play sometimes and your constant swearing and use of foul language is not suitable for children to hear. When you stop swearing, then you can meet them.' 'It makes people feel very tense and upset when you talk to them about being controlled by things from outer space. Maybe you should only stay with us while you can talk about other things, and go off to your own room when these thoughts become overwhelming.' Close friends and family may learn in time to cope with behaviour that is strange without it troubling them unduly, but there will always be those who cannot or acquaintances from whom less can be expected. Education about schizophrenia is a great help as the more people understand the nature of the problem and what is likely to happen, the more easily they will learn to cope.

If you are out with the sufferer who starts acting oddly for whatever reason, there is possibly little else to be done other than to avoid drawing attention to the behaviour, by acting calmly, reasonably and, if necessary, quickly, to get the sufferer out of the situation. It can distress sufferers when they are well to know that they have been seen, by neighbours, acquaintances or just people in the street, acting in a peculiar manner when they are not well. In such cases you are being fair and protecting the sufferer by removing him from the public gaze. Other things, such as odd movements or twitches, which are fairly constant behaviour, you may simply have to get used to and accept as part of the person, and ignore when you are out. If other people are rude enough to stare, that is their problem and there is little you can do about it.

Worry and Anxiety
Many of the worries, fears and anxieties that you have as the relative of a schizophrenic may be quite realistic and justified. Worrying alone, however, will accomplish little, if anything. Part of the solution lies in facing what the worries are and what, if anything, can be done about them. If nothing can be done, that must be acknowledged.

What will happen when I die?
A common worry of most parents is what is going to happen to the sufferer when they are either too old or infirm to cope or when they die. This is a very real problem, since there is no reason why the sufferer should not outlive his parents.

It helps to discuss this in a calm and reasonable manner with both the sufferer and the family members. It is something that almost certainly everyone will have thoughts of at some time, but they may be too embarrassed or think it too morbid to bring up. Discuss with siblings how much they might help, whether the sufferer could live with them all or some of the time. Ask the sufferer what he would prefer. Sheltered accommodation might be a possibility, but might require some investigation ahead of time. Maybe the only sort of accommodation available requires the sufferer to have a number of self-help skills. Does he have these? If not, what can be done to teach him? In some instances, as parents get older, it may be better for the patient to move into such accommodation, if it is available, before it is strictly necessary. Visits home can be frequent and the transition may be easier when it does not immediately follow the death or sudden illness of the parent who has been caring for him until then.

In some cases it is the sufferer who cares for the elderly parents, doing things for them, whilst getting emotional and psychological support from them. Again the question should be, where is this support going to come from after the parents' death?

Where the family lives in rented property, enquiries should be made as to whether the sufferer will be able to become the tenant after the parents' death. Where the parents have property and money to leave, care should be taken to safeguard the sufferer's interests when making a will. A solicitor will be able to help you with this. It should be possible to leave money to the sufferer in a trust of some form, so that he has money to pay for his daily living needs but cannot spend everything in one irresponsible spending spree when he is not well.

Beyond taking all the sensible measures that you can, there is nothing to be done. Dying is inevitable and you can waste a great deal of time, energy and emotion worrying about what will happen when you are gone, and miss out on some of the things you could be doing together in the present.

Will It Happen to Me?
This tends to be a fear of younger family members, be they siblings or offspring of the sufferer. The closer the blood tie to the schizophrenic person the higher the risk, but bear in mind that the vast *majority* of relatives of a schizophrenic are *not* themselves schizophrenic. A talk with a psychiatrist who knows something about the genetics of schizophrenia may help to assess any possible risks.

The same is true where a couple are worried about risks to any children they might have. The risk comes not just from any inherited predisposition, but also from the environment. A child brought up in a family where every move he makes is being assessed as to whether it is 'normal' or not, or to whether he is 'turning out like his uncle' or 'going funny' is unlikely to grow up to be an entirely happy and psychologically healthy child, whether or not he develops schizophrenia.

Priorities

Strain in the family is likely to stem from many sources, but can provide an additional burden when it is couched in terms of, 'You are not being fair . . .' The family as a whole, or a particular member of it, often a mother or a wife, may fall into the habit of always putting the sufferer first. Yes, he is the one with the most problems; yes, others do have to put themselves out for him, but not always, not every time. It is easy to think you are doing the right, the caring, thing by insisting that siblings include the sufferer in their plans but they *do* have the right to their own, independent life, without always having someone else, whether well or ill, along. Not only should the children be able to do things on their own, it can also be helpful for them to have areas of interest with each parent which do not include the sufferer, so that they have a chance to develop a full relationship of their own with the parent, without the sufferer's influence and interference.

Refusing to go out because they 'should' stay in with the sufferer becomes a habit, even when it is possible to leave him, or to get another relative or friend to stay in with him. Even if, at the end, you choose to sacrifice your life entirely to that of the sufferer it is unlikely to make things very much better and you certainly cannot force this solution on others. A husband who feels he is being pushed out because of an ill child may literally leave; siblings who feel they are being ignored or neglected may get into various sorts of trouble in order to win back some of their parents' care and attention. Often the choices are heart-breakingly difficult to make. In the case of a young wife with children where the husband becomes ill and is at home, withdrawn and unmotivated, it might be that the best thing for the husband is for the wife to stay with him and do all she can for him; but the best thing for the children might be for the wife to leave him and concentrate her time and energies on herself and her children.

These sorts of problems should be discussed with the sufferer's doctor, but bear in mind that in most cases his first concern will be for the sufferer's welfare. You also need to have someone who is representing your interests to talk to. In the last instance though, this, like all very difficult and personal problems, can only be solved by you.

Acceptance

Possibly the hardest thing for a relative to achieve is acceptance — acceptance that there is no quick, easy answer, acceptance that for some things there is no answer at all, or that *all* the alternatives are unacceptable. The cry that 'there *must* be something else', 'there *must* be a better way', is probably felt by all relatives at some time, and probably by most professionals as well. Sometimes there is but sometimes there simply is not, and it is better for all concerned to face this. Time, money, energy and emotion can all be wasted. Sometimes the only solution is to accept that the world is imperfect, that there are not, for example, enough services and then look for a different type of solution which might, for example, involve working politically for a better deal for community support services. Sadly people can waste a lot of money they can ill afford chasing a miracle cure, be it vitamins or courses to improve self-confidence.

Chapter 11, on getting help, may help to clarify in your own mind what it is you want, and whether it is realistic. *All* of us, whether we are a sufferer, relative or professional, *want* a miracle cure. Only those of us who accept that one does not exist can then move on to make the very best of what we have got.

9.

SUFFERERS' PROBLEMS

The problems that a sufferer from schizophrenia experiences fall into three broad areas. Firstly, there are those which are directly linked to the illness and its symptoms, including residual psychotic symptoms and behaviour, withdrawal, apathy and difficulty in concentrating and dealing with the environment so as to minimize relapse. The second group of problems can be broadly defined as dealing with, and living as a member of, a family. The last category involves difficulties in living as a member of the community and the prejudices of society against, and stereotypes of, the mentally ill. Problems of illness behaviour will be dealt with in the next chapter and those of minimizing relapses in Chapter 12. This chapter is concerned with the sufferer's problems in dealing with others and the feelings to which this might give rise.

Living with the Family
Relatives are not the only people to feel the strain of living with a recovering schizophrenic patient. The sufferer also has to adjust to the situation, his illness and the changes in him and his new position in the family.

Talking to relatives
As a sufferer you may now find a barrier between yourself and other members of the family. The experiences that have been part of the illness episode often seem so bizarre that there is a degree of embarrassment in talking about them. *You* do not understand why you felt or believed such strange things, so how can anybody else? Although endless talking about or analysing what happened to you, and what it means, is not usually very profitable, some brief explanation to relatives can be helpful. Their only understanding of the illness is what they see, how they see

you behave and this is a very different concept of the illness from yours. To explain how or why you behaved as you did, or why something was so important to you, may go a long way toward helping deal with other problems. To learn that what seemed totally irrational to them had meaning for you at the time, helps to put the behaviour into perspective.

Because of strange and seemingly irrational requests in the past, relatives may require more persuading or explanation now than they did before you were ill. Although this can be very frustrating and irritating to you, from the relatives' point of view it is understandable. Try to give them the reassurance they need, that you know what you are doing when you really do! Impatience on both sides can lead to arguments, bitterness and an exacerbation of problems.

Dependency

The sufferer often becomes dependent on the relatives with whom he lives in a wide range of ways. Whether living with parents or a spouse the sufferer may rely on others to provide the bulk of his daily comforts, from providing meals, doing the washing and providing a clean and comfortable house to live in, to being the only source of contact with the outside world. The ability which those involved need in order to cope with such dependency is affected not only by what is involved, but also by the nature of the relationship.

Spouses may feel that the sufferer has become another child for them to look after, rather than an equal partner in the marriage, and may resent this deeply. They have lost the person with whom they used to share problems as well as dreams. Now, instead of having someone to lean on, on occasions, they are in the position of having to provide continual support. Although sufferers can be aware of how much they rely on their spouse, they frequently do not realize the immense strain it is putting on that person and the relationship.

The nature of the dependency relationship in a parental family is very different. Often the adult child has not left home before he becomes ill, or has only left to go to college or university. His base is still with his parents. Even where he has been living away from home it may not have been for very long, and in a flat with friends, rather than a 'home of his own'. Even the most stable and independent of offspring remain children to their parents long after they have reached adulthood; parents find it difficult to accept the adult child's ability to be responsible for himself. When someone is ill, and clearly not responsible or able to take responsibility, parents again take over. Although some find the strain great, many are not even aware of how much they do. If mother has always provided meals, cleaned the house, washed clothes, she continues to do so, often not being aware of the effect this might have on her child. When the child is ill such behaviour may be necessary, but as he becomes well again parents should encourage the sufferer to become as independent as he can. It may not be possible for the person to live alone, or be truly independent, but neither will he learn how to make decisions and take responsibility for himself it he is not given the opportunity to try.

This is often a double problem as the sufferer may not *want* to take this responsibility, and may need persuading into doing things for himself. At times it may even seem cruel or not worth the effort. A different problem occurs when parents do not realize what they are doing, or believe it to be the best thing for the sufferer, that they are protecting him from unnecessary stress. What is important in both cases are the long-term consequences of this dependency. Parents will not always be there and the more independent the sufferer is, the more he can care and make decisions for himself, the less he will be likely to require institutional or supervisory care when they are no longer there.

The myth of the 'before' person

Schizophrenia changes people, of that there is no doubt. Many sufferers are aware that they are not the same person they were before the illness struck, that they cannot do the same things. Concentration is often poor, talking to people difficult and finding the energy to do anything almost impossible.

This awareness can be made very much more acute by relatives' attitudes. Some relatives will often tell the sufferer that he has changed, he is not like he was before, that they do not know him any more, that he is no longer their child, that he has become a 'stranger'. In asking relatives to describe the sufferer's personality I have been asked frequently 'Do you mean as he is now, or as he used to be?', even if 'as he used to be' is twenty or thirty years ago. This attitude can lead to two different problems for the sufferer.

Firstly, it may be that any changes he makes, any improvements in his condition, are either not noticed or not valued very highly by the family. In any circumstances it is often difficult to see changes in a person you are living with until something happens to cause a reassessment. Relatives may note 'He is so much better than he used to be', often meaning that major psychotic symptoms have disappeared, or that someone is now quiet and fairly docile, rather than noisy and difficult to live with. If relatives are always looking back to the sufferer's 'old self' they will not notice small improvements. It can be very disheartening, even when they are noticed, to be told 'That's all very well, but . . .' especially if the change or new behaviour has involved the sufferer in making a lot of effort and for him it resembles a remarkable achievement. If the sufferer's efforts are either unnoticed, or belittled, it is little wonder that many stop trying.

The second problem has more to do with the way the sufferer sees himself. To be told that 'you are not the person you were' would lead even the most sane to doubt their own experiences and perceptions. Aware of changes, even possibly of being controlled by forces outside himself, nevertheless the sufferer is fighting to retain his own identity. Meanwhile the relatives are trying, although not intentionally, to convince him that he *is* a different person and, furthermore, they do not really like this new person. It is hardly surprising that many sufferers have problems knowing who they are.

As a relative you may justifiably feel that you have lost someone and may need to mourn this loss, but it should not take place in front of the person whose loss you regret. The sufferer needs to know that he is accepted with the family *as he is now*, not simply because of what he once was. This might mean accepting limitations in the sufferer's behaviour and involvement in the family. It should not, however, mean that aggressive or antisocial behaviour is unconditionally accepted, but that the *person* is, despite such behaviour.

Living in Society

If living in the family is sometimes hard work, living in society as 'a mental patient' or 'an ex-mental patient' is often harder. Many people are frightened of such individuals, and society as a whole seems prejudiced against them. This can aggravate problems the sufferer already has, such as difficulties in making friends or finding suitable employment. But the feeling of being stigmatized by the label 'mental patient' or 'schizophrenic' is a more general one; it can result in a sufferer feeling extremely isolated from other people, embarrassed or ashamed of what has happened to him and anxious that others should not know.

How a sufferer and his relatives deal with this depends on many factors, some of which will be discussed in the next chapter, and some of which have already been mentioned in Chapter 7.

10.

MANAGING COMMON PROBLEMS

Before considering some common problems which families who have a schizophrenic person living with them have to face, it will be useful to consider some general strategies of management and factors which affect all our behaviour and the ways we can change it.

Guidelines for Change

Reinforcement
Much of our behaviour is governed by its consequences. If something pleasant (or rewarding) happens we are most likely to repeat that behaviour, and if something unpleasant (or punishing) happens we are less likely to repeat it. This sounds like common sense, but that does not detract from its importance; it is something we often neglect in everyday life, but these are crucial elements of behaviour therapy. It sounds easy and straightforward enough in theory, but in practice it is not always so simple. It means that if you reward or praise someone for doing something it should be wholehearted, with no qualifications. It is all too easy to say 'That's good, but . . .' and then qualify your praise, by saying something like 'Why didn't you do . . .' or 'It would have been better if . . .' or 'I would have . . .' This can negate the effect of the praise entirely.

Reinforcement should also be as close in time as possible to the behaviour being encouraged and, if necessary, a statement of what you are pleased about. So, for example, if you are trying to encourage the sufferer to take a greater pride in his appearance, comment positively on this but give specific instances of what is good, or what you are especially pleased about; rather than just saying 'You look nice', add a positive comment on the fact that he is wearing clean clothes or has shaved or whatever is most appropriate.

Being constant in your response
This is particularly important, and often extremely difficult. Sometimes people do odd things because of the attention it gets them, or some other positive effect. To change this sort of behaviour means shifting attention away from it, and on to something else that is normal and acceptable. However, if this is going to work, then once the decision has been made to change the pattern of reinforcement this must be strictly adhered to. Any lapses make the situation worse because they convince the person that they just have to keep on for a bit longer and you will give in again.

Small steps
It is usually very difficult for anyone to make big, sudden changes in their behaviour. Any task needs to be broken down into a series of small tasks or steps, and these completed (and rewarded) separately. It is often helpful to start at the finish of the chain of tasks. So, for example, if you are trying to encourage someone who does nothing to help with the household chores, it might be too much to expect them to vacuum his room immediately; but you could start by getting him to put the vacuum cleaner away for you, and then once this is done regularly gradually add more to it. Change will not come about overnight. The new behaviour must be repeated over and over and again until it becomes automatic, or a new habit.

Putting it all together
How does this work in practice? Let us return to the problem of the person who will not get up for breakfast. The simple solution is not to take meals to him in bed. If he wants to eat, he gets up and eats with everybody else, not special meals at special times. The exception to this might be if family members going to work have breakfast *very* early, or if everybody has breakfast at different times because of work schedules.

Things will probably change slowly, particularly if the habit is well established. Someone who has been getting up at eleven o'clock for years is unlikely to switch suddenly to eight-thirty with no problems. Maybe, for a while, meals will have to be served when the person gets up, making it a little earlier each week. For a while the person may eat breakfast and go back to bed. Bear with this.

Approximations to what you want should be recognized and rewarded as the person *is* making an effort. Recognize this, and recognize how hard this may be for him. Nagging now will not help at all, and may only be counter-productive. Make compromises, be prepared to adapt, do not simply expect all the changes to come from the person you have defined as 'the problem'.

This type of solution may result in a battle of wills for a few days and it is important to: (1) spell out exactly what you are doing, and why, to both sufferer and the rest of the family; (2) be consistent — if you give in once you make the problem worse; (3) get the family's co-operation — with no one sneaking him in odd snacks or cups of tea; and (4) inform the psychiatrist or other staff what you are doing.

Dealing with Symptoms

Usually drugs are the best method of dealing with psychotic behaviour and if one drug does not suppress the symptoms, it is often useful to try another type. Be guided by your psychiatrist in this and do not give up on drugs just because the first does not have the desired effect. I stress the importance of persevering with medication because *nothing* else has the same effect on the psychotic symptoms. Where these persist in the face of medication there is, sadly, very often little else that can be done. Trying to change psychotic symptoms by behavioural or psychological methods is extremely difficult, if not impossible. It is very time-consuming, slow, potentially harmful work and should be left to professionals. However, the behaviour still needs managing on a day-to-day basis.

Delusions and hallucinations

Dealing with these has already been mentioned in Chapter 7. To sum up, probably the best solution is to maintain a stable, calm front in the face of someone talking about odd ideas, to state your own position clearly and firmly and to refuse to be drawn into a discussion or argument about it. Distraction sometimes works, involving the sufferer in something else, especially if it involves some sort of activity.

If the sufferer has very loosely associated ideas, and often loses the thread of his own conversation, it is sometimes possible to slowly change the track of the conversation and wean the sufferer on to another, safer subject.

Aggression, violence and hostility

Although many people are worried about a schizophrenic person being violent this is rarely the case. It is unfortunate that a few of those who do become aggressive and violent are spectacularly so, and it is these who make the newspaper headlines. Sometimes a patient becomes violent as a result of delusions or hallucinations, and believes that he is acting as reality dictates. Sometimes the aggression is not the direct result of a delusion or hallucination, but comes about indirectly because the sufferer becomes frightened and agitated by what is happening to him. Aggression or violence of this type should always be reported to a doctor, and may require changes in medication.

Usually, however, aggressive outbursts are of short duration and happen when the sufferer feels under pressure of some sort. He may feel he is being constantly supervised, or manipulated by the family, or that they are always critical or demanding too much of him. If the sufferer becomes agitated or hostile try to remain calm, and avoid arguing or counter-attacking. Threats of reprisals or counter attacks should *never* be used, nor should the police, doctors or return to hospital be used as threats of control. If the sufferer is frightened by his own behaviour, then try to reassure him that no one is going to harm him and that help is available. Since the people who live with the sufferer are emotionally involved, they often handle such outbursts badly. Calling in someone else whom the sufferer knows and trusts might ease the tension; this might be the GP, a minister, or another relative or close friend living nearby. Often such people do not need to do anything. Simply by being present they can reduce the emotional tone of the atmosphere. The sufferer may be able to go to his own room and recover his self-control whilst the third party waits with the relative. The aim is to try to defuse the situation without damage being done. This includes damage to the relationship between the sufferer and his relative, which frequently receives a setback as the result of such outbursts.

Safety is the first consideration in violent outbursts, the safety of both the relatives and the sufferer. Elderly relatives, female relatives or children may feel most frightened and threatened by an aggressive outburst. Relatives should try to avoid becoming isolated with the sufferer who has aggressive tendencies. If you are alone with someone who becomes violent, your first priority should be to ensure your own safety and to get away. I have heard one mother say that she keeps a bucket of cold water handy; throwing this over her son when he becomes violent slows him down enough for her to make her escape. Tactics such as this need to be employed with caution. If you *do not* get away you may have to deal with someone who is very much angrier.

The same is true if you are going to try to restrain someone. Make sure there are enough people to hold on to someone (sitting on them is a method that some people find the most useful) while one goes for help, or until the aggressive outburst is over.

Such measures may seem cruel, but may be a less drastic alternative than the consequences of violence. Any tactics you do use, be it cold water, sitting on someone, or going for help, should be explained and discussed *before* use with the sufferer. Many sufferers will agree that no matter how unpleasant any tactics might be, including calling the police, this is preferable to them hurting someone. If the violence happens unexpectedly and you have not been able to discuss it beforehand it is especially important to talk about what happened afterwards and explain why you behaved as you did. Many sufferers do not realize how much they can frighten their relatives, particularly if they are frightened themselves. Outbursts should be reported to the doctor, particularly if they are more frequent than extremely rare, since increases in medication may help the problem.

Dealing with less serious outbursts may be possible without having to call in outside help. When the sufferer is well such outbursts should be mentioned and limits set. Make it clear then what is acceptable and what is not, and agree on this. Then, in difficult times, these need repeating firmly and with no change. Emphasize that there is a limit to what you will put up with.

Some behaviours are acceptable and others are not, and everyone should be clear on what is and what is not permissible. For example, you may decide that throwing objects around the home is not acceptable, but punching a pillow or mattress in his own room is. Whether and how you will put up with someone screaming and being verbally insulting and abusive in private is up to you, but it should be stressed that it is unacceptable in public.

I feel strongly that physical violence should not be tolerated whatever the circumstances.

If the sufferer is out of control, and seems unable to regain control you should leave him alone, preferably leaving the house. Sometimes this space allows the sufferer to regain control. If, after a reasonable time, the sufferer has not regained control other people may need to be called in, either the GP, psychiatrist or police. If the patient seems actively dangerous, either to himself or others, they should be called immediately. When contacting the police explain about the patient's condition and illness, warn them of his likely behaviour and response to them, and the reasons for it. Some police officers are very good at dealing with such incidents, although sadly not all. If they can come with the doctor this sometimes helps. Embarrassment or shame at needing to involve the police should never stop you calling them. Your first priority should be everyone's safety.

Many relatives do not like the idea of calling in the police because of previous unpleasant experiences or because they have heard that the police may not be very understanding. Although in some cases the police do arrive in largish numbers and use what seems to be disproportionate amounts of force, this has to be weighed against the probable outcomes if you do not call them. Where there is a real physical danger to others, it is probably better to risk a bad experience with the police than it is to have someone hurt. Injuring others will usually lead to the patient being put under section, or, depending on the severity of the injury, being sent to a State Hospital or even prison.

It is sad to have to acknowledge that for problems like violence all the solutions are potentially unpleasant, but then violence itself is unpleasant. Although a person's violence may be seen to have mitigating circumstances in that they have schizophrenia, this does not stop the violence hurting others. Protection of yourself and other family members, the public as a whole, as well as the sufferer, has to be a priority.

Depression
Depression sometimes forms part of the schizophrenic illness, but often is a reaction to it. As the sufferer comes to realize what has happened to him, or the changes which the illness has brought to his life, and as he contemplates a future not knowing what might happen, depression is often the logical outcome.

It is not always easy for relatives to recognize depression for what it is. It is not just someone sitting around feeling sad and unhappy and crying a lot. These may be features of behaviour in some depressed people, but more importantly depression is to do with feeling helpless and hopeless, inadequate to deal with the situation. These, together with feelings of guilt, self-recrimination, self-blame and worthlessness, are central to depression, but often remain unexpressed. Rather than talk about his feelings the depressed person is more likely to show behaviour patterns of listlessness, apathy and withdrawal, insomnia or waking very early in the morning, and loss of appetite (or in some cases, particularly women, over-eating). Since the apathy and withdrawal are often part of the schizophrenic experience anyway, depression may be missed.

Drugs may help to relieve the depression in some instances but since they will not cure the schizophrenia, where depression is a response to that, it will continue when the drugs are stopped. The sufferer needs professional help and advice in coming to terms with his changed situation, coping with his problems and planning for the future.

One thing relatives can do is to be patient. Show support, caring and acceptance, just by being with the person if necessary, for it is unlikely that the sufferer will be able to discuss his feelings with you. Nor can he 'snap out of it' or 'pull himself together' and to say that he should will only add to the sufferer's burden. He would if he could, but he simply cannot. It is important not to let yourself be drawn into the sufferer's helpless and hopeless frame of mind. Even if you feel this at times, now is *not* the time to discuss it with him. Be positive, but understanding, make it clear that you are planning for the future and wait. Many depressions are self-limiting, and the patient will move through this period. This does not mean it can be ignored since much damage can be done to the sufferer, the family and their relationship in the meantime.

If the sufferer is depressed he is unlikely to try or be able to hide it from the doctors, and it should be picked up by them, but if you do not think they are taking it seriously then point out the behaviour that worries you to the psychiatrist.

Suicide

Any fears that you have that the sufferer may be thinking of suicide should always be reported to the psychiatrist or GP, together with the evidence you have for your fears. The talk may not always be direct but vague and along with lines of 'I can't see any reason to go on'. Although suicide among schizophrenics is not very common it does happen, and some patients are more vulnerable to this than others.

Suicide attempts do not appear to be related to any particular phase of the illness, and depend largely on the nature and course that the illness takes in the individual. It may be related to the fear and anxiety that accompany the sufferer's feelings of loss of control of himself. Or it may accompany the realization of illness, but not the acceptance of it. The feeling of hopelessness that is part of depression may make nonsense of someone's previous ability to accept and cope with the illness. A few patients have voices that tell them to kill themselves or suggest it indirectly by stressing the person's worthlessness. Occasionally the person's delusions about themselves may cause them to try to commit suicide to 'prove' that they are immortal, or indestructible. In these cases suicide attempts will be limited to the occurrence of these acute symptoms.

When a sufferer talks seriously of suicide, hospitalization may not always be necessary but in many instances the doctors will think that at least some form of constant observation is necessary. In some cases when a person is able to talk of such thoughts it means that he is in more control of them, and therefore less likely to act impulsively. If a person is very depressed he may not have the physical or mental energy to try to commit suicide and, paradoxically, this may only happen as he begins to improve. If the sufferer talks to you of suicide then it is important that, above all else, you remain calm. Listen to what he says, showing that you are taking him seriously, and that you appreciate his trust in you in telling you of his feelings. If the sufferer has been through this before, it may help to talk about this, reminding him that these feelings have passed before. Even if the sufferer does not make any suicide attempt, having to listen to him talking of such things is very distressing. As well as confiding your anxieties about the sufferer's possible behaviour to his doctor, it is important that you have someone to listen to your worries at such a time.

Social Behaviour and Relationships
Difficulties in interacting with other people and forming

relationships are probably the most common problems that the schizophrenic person has to deal with. They are also problems which cause relatives much distress because, in many cases, they are the most obvious manifestation of the schizophrenia. They are an important category of problems because they interrelate with so many others. It is not just a question of being lonely because it affects the individual's ability to care for himself (for example, if he cannot shop because he cannot deal with shop assistants), to enjoy much of his leisure time and even to work.

The difficulties experienced in social behaviour are, as in other things, a varied group. They range from total withdrawal and a denial of wanting any interaction to a desire to interact but an anxiety or inability about doing so, to inappropriate behaviour in public which makes others avoid him and family or friends embarrassed to go out with him.

In many cases it seems that the anxiety and withdrawal stem from a loss of confidence which follows the schizophrenic experience. Confidence can be encouraged and reinstated by gradually introducing the sufferer to social events and preparing him well (and possibly others involved) so that the occasions are seen as 'successes'. Preventing failure is all important here. Success can be aided by telling the sufferer what is going on. For example, if friends are coming to the house, tell him who is coming, why (if there is any particular reason) and how long they are likely to stay. This information can be supplemented by suggestions of what they are interested in and might like to talk about (e.g., ask them about their recent holiday). Sufferers often find it easier to be a listener than do a lot of talking; if they can become adept at asking the right sort of questions, showing interest, and prompting people to 'tell me more about that, it sounds fascinating' they can be regarded by others as good conversationalists without ever having said much!

Other behaviour may also need some prompting and guidelines. For example, you could suggest that the sufferer comes to the front door with you to see people off, or say that if you leave the room for any reason he is not being deserted, you will be back as soon as possible, and he is to carry on the conversation whilst you are away. Visiting other people or other places can be dealt with in the same way. Try to give helpful information that the sufferer can use to deal with the unfamiliar. If the sufferer has particular anxieties, like feeling trapped, then calmly point

out the exits to him and then ignore the subject. If the sufferer
has any tendency to anxiety or panic attacks in social or public
settings it is also useful to know where the lavatories are (and
not only for obvious reasons!). If the sufferer finds that the
situation is becoming more than he can deal with he can make
a discreet escape to the nearest lavatory where he can be alone
for a few minutes to gain control of his emotions.

It is often helpful at first to make visits fairly short and for the
sufferer to be able to leave reasonably early when he wants.
Knowing he can leave at any time often makes it easier to stay,
whereas knowing he has to sit through a two-hour film, for
example, may increase restlessness.

It can also be helpful to tell friends or relatives what they might
expect from the sufferer, since if they are prepared they are more
likely to cope well with the situation and not become
embarrassed, especially if the sufferer is apt to lapse into long
periods of silence. They may be worried that this is a response
to something they have done or said, and they may fear that they
have made the situation worse. It is easier to believe that they
have not created the situation if they are told beforehand that
it might happen. It often helps to remember that schizophrenic
individuals tend to have a slow response time, that is, they take
longer to reply than is usual. It often helps a conversation to wait
just that bit longer than you would normally expect to.

Friends are often wary of involving the sufferer in things he
used to do before he became ill, of asking him to help generally
or do things for them. This often stems from a misplaced sense
of protection. Encourage them to include the sufferer when they
normally would have done so, and especially if they feel that he
can help.

If the patient has no friends then setting out to make them can
be very hard work indeed. It is important that neither relative
nor sufferer should build their expectations up too high. Finding
friends is not something that happens instantaneously. Joining
clubs or groups may be useful. There are organizations for
psychiatric patients and although the sufferer may have some
resistance to joining a club full of other people with problems,
it can be a helpful first step, especially if he has a residue of
symptoms and behavioural problems. These might be tolerated
better amongst such a group.

In the early stages of becoming resocialized, simply getting used to having people about, especially strangers, is important. To this end evening classes can serve a useful function. Although usually put forward as a way of meeting people and making friends they are not always as good from this point of view as one might suppose. Most of the time is spent listening to the lecturer or concentrating on the task in hand (depending on what you are studying) and there is usually only limited time for interaction with other people. Some people make a real effort to talk to others, but there is seen to be nothing odd in the people who sit quietly, taking in what goes on around them, a role that most sufferers could easily fit into. A word of caution though. The exercise will probably be more successful if the sufferer picks a subject he has an interest in, whether or not he knows anything about it, and goes to a class which is for 'interest only' rather than having an exam at the end of it. This is needless stress for the sufferer to start with, although he may want to take classes that will improve his job prospects at a later stage. Some subjects will require the students to work on their own during the week between classes. The sufferer should only start a class of this type if he is *sure* that he will do the work. If he does not he will fall behind and will not understand the weekly classes, which will cause stress and frustration, leading to him dropping out of the class and a subsequent sense of failure.

There should be little worry about being able to concentrate for the length of time involved, since after a busy day few people can concentrate for a couple of hours. In this respect the sufferer will find his wandering attention little different from anybody else's. As long as it does not cause him to become restless this should not be a problem. If the sufferer is very anxious about attending somewhere on his own for the first time it can help if a friend or relative can go with him the first few times. This support can be gradually withdrawn as the sufferer gains in confidence.

Another source of friendship is a penpal. For some reason many sufferers from schizophrenia write a lot of letters. This can be harnessed into a rewarding correspondence and friendship with others, without the emotional strain of a face-to-face confrontation. There are various organizations for finding penfriends and some magazines carry advertisements either for penfriends or the agencies. If the sufferer would prefer to correspond with someone in the same position as himself then organizations such as the National Schizophrenia Fellowship may be able to help.

Withdrawal

So far we have been considering the shy and withdrawn sufferer from the point of view of encouraging him to socialize more. It should, however, be borne in mind that withdrawal can be a protective feature for many sufferers who find it a way of dealing with unacceptable levels of tension and anxiety. On occasions this must be respected. The sufferer has his own rights to privacy and to be alone. The sufferer will sometimes find it easier to accept company and social interaction if he also knows that he has somewhere he can go to be alone and where this will be respected, at least for a time. This relieves some of the pressure on him. As in many areas of schizophrenia, there is a fine line to be drawn between too much withdrawal, which can turn into apathy and inertia, and too much social and emotional pressure, which can lead to relapse. The balance is different for every patient and can only be gauged individually over time.

Rejection

One crucial factor for relatives and friends to bear in mind is that at times the sufferer is going to reject them, their offers of help, their concern and support. Knowing this in advance can minimize the hurt felt, but it will still be there. It is important to remember that such rejection is not usually personal but stems from the sufferer's own problems, his difficulty in relating to other people and thus accepting anything from them. Friends and relatives must learn to accept the rejection without hostility and continue to make overtures towards the sufferer because sometimes they *will* be accepted, and at such times the sufferer may be able to tell you how much he appreciates the continued offer of support.

Work

Whether the sufferer can continue to work depends not only on how well he recovers from the acute schizophrenic episode and the type of problems he is left with, but also on the type of working and training he had before the illness, his expectations about returning to work and the state of the job market itself.

Both relatives and sufferers as well as professionals often see 'going back to work' or 'getting a job' as the goal of treatment or the thing which marks the sufferer as 'well' or recovered. The equation, however, is not so simple, and each case must be judged separately. As in most things there are advantages and disadvantages in returning to work, which much be considered carefully.

Returning to work can be very important in helping the person feel that he has recovered, is 'normal' again, since this is behaviour expected of 'normal' people. Unemployment only serves to emphasize the difference from everyone else. Possibly the only positive thing about high unemployment figures is that it puts less pressure on those who are unable to work through mental illness to explain why they are not working.

Being at work also provides 'something to do' and a reason for getting up and getting dressed each day; it provides a routine and a way of measuring and accounting for the passage of time. An important factor is that it takes the person out of the house and away from relatives for part of each day. In itself this might be one of the most important reasons for finding a job. Both parties benefit from this time apart and relatives particularly feel a sense of release and freedom. They have some time on their own to pursue their own interests, and tolerance is often easier when it only has to be for a few hours in the evening rather than all day as well. Lastly, for a family with financial difficulties through being on a low, fixed income, the money to be earned may be of particular importance.

Against these benefits must be weighed some of the problems that might result from working. The stress of working may be too much for some sufferers. Even if the job itself is seen as 'non-stressful' it must be understood that there are factors inherent in working itself which might make it very difficult and very stressful for some patients. Among these are the daily nature of work, the fact that you cannot not go if you 'don't feel like it', the need to be punctual and the need to work for specific hours. In essence, to be at work consistently and reliably can be a strain for some sufferers.

Most jobs involve at least some element of working with others, and even a low level of socializing and having to communicate with other people may prove beyond the ability of some people. This sensitivity and/or suspiciousness may lead them to misinterpret criticism about their work, or the normal joking and teasing that happens amongst workmates.

There are some specific areas that might cause problems at work, or make the sufferer unsuitable for certain types of work.

Concentration
Many sufferers complain of an inability to concentrate. Some find that this can be overcome when they are doing something they want to do, are interested in and which holds their attention, but not in other tasks. So, for example, a sufferer may be able to concentrate on a game of chess, but not enough to carry out routine tasks at work. Although repetitive tasks might seem helpful for those with concentration problems, often the reverse is true and the very repetition adds to the difficulty in keeping attention on the task.

Some people do manage to develop a few tricks of their own to help concentration but these are highly idiosyncratic and there is not a lot that seems to help the problem.

Expectations and qualifications
Schizophrenics often find themselves unable to carry out the jobs they trained for, or which they expected to do, before they became ill. Limitations in concentration, an inability to cope with the job responsibilities or to be quickly decisive, a general slowness, or an unwillingness to communicate may all mean that sufferers end up doing fairly menial work, well below their qualifications. This may cause intense frustration and a feeling that working at all is pointless. The sufferer needs a lot of understanding and help to deal with these problems and to come to accept them.

It is not only the job itself which may prove frustrating, but the people the sufferer now works with may come from a very different background with different interests. This may make the sufferer feel even more 'different' or alienated. Young sufferers in particular, with little experience of others' lifestyles, may be critical and intolerant of others; this can lead to arguments with workmates which in turn push the sufferer to the edge of the group and increase his isolation from his fellow workers. This can sometimes be alleviated by allowing the sufferer some small degree of 'moaning' at home, and making sure that he has the time and encouragement to engage in his preferred interests, preferably with someone. Tolerance and understanding of other people's lifestyles should be encouraged, possibly being seen as an educative exercise. Having something to talk about in common with them often helps, and here television programmes can be useful.

Sometimes sufferers may think they are capable of more than they really are. Whilst encouraging them to do something at which they will fail should be avoided, letting them apply for jobs for which they are not suited is not always a bad thing. In these days of high unemployment they are highly unlikely to get the job, but they may feel they are doing something or at least 'trying' by applying. The point at which this stops being encouraging and starts becoming depressing and dispiriting will vary between individuals.

Communication

Sensitivity or suspicion may make schizophrenics poor at understanding what is needed or expected of them. Instructions at work (or elsewhere) must be clear, straightforward and unambiguous. Preferably they should be given simply and assimilated into a routine. Writing things down serves as a memory aid to many sufferers, and if they get confused they can consult a clear list of thing they have to do. If they have any doubt they should be able to check with the superior and, if possible, check the written list.

Response to workmates

Inevitably the sufferer will act strangely at work at some time. How this is dealt with by workmates will depend, to some extent, on how well they know the sufferer and like him, and how much they know about his problems. Someone who acts oddly out-of-the-blue can appear very frightening to those who do not know what is going on and whose behaviour has come as a total surprise. Unexpected and unprovoked anger, laughter or other emotion can be extremely confusing and disturbing for workmakes to deal with. Unreliability will often cause irritation in others, whether this is in the form of walking out midway through something, being unpunctual or not turning up. General slowness or an inability to take any initiative may also cause irritability, frustration or anger on the part of co-workers. The more the sufferer's behaviour affects their ability to do their job or causes them to do work for him, the more likely they are to become angry and to complain, either to him or to superiors. This will put more stress on the sufferer and may cause his behaviour to become even more disturbed.

These problems should be talked out at home and, if possible, with appropriate people at work, be that the immediate supervisor, a higher manager or boss, or even trade union officials. In some instances a change of job may be required, for example where work on a production line is being held up by a sufferer's inability to work up to speed.

What type of work?
An atmosphere of support and acceptance, where fluctuations in behaviour and performance are accepted, would be ideal but is unlikely to be found. Even without the ideal a set routine is probably important, but not constant repetition which causes boredom and may aggravate concentration problems. Limited change is also important. Inevitably there will be change at work, but there are areas where equipment, routine and environment remain constant over long periods of time. Change can also apply to workmates, and a high staff turnover can prove very stressful to a sufferer. A low involvement with others and a fairly stable workforce may be helpful. A low level of responsibility is usually an important feature, which includes not having to make decisions or supervise the work of others.

Part-time work, if it is available, may be appropriate; the sufferer may cope with job conditions and stresses for half a day, or two or three days a week, with which he could not deal on a full-time basis. Although in some instances part-time work can be a period of readjustment, and allow the sufferer to move on to full-time work, sometimes this is not possible. When the sufferer has reached a position with which he can cope and from which he gets some satisfaction, it is important not to push him further until he is confronted by something which causes him to fail or have a relapse.

What to tell them at work
Chapter 7 deals with telling people about the illness and what you choose to tell the people you work with is up to you. There is, however, one category which is different. If you are asked officially if you have ever had any mental illness or treatment for mental illness and you deny this, then you might leave yourself open to dismissal if the facts ever come to light and it is thought that the illness might affect your ability to do the job. Although some people do lie, and apparently successfully, the knowledge

of the lie and the strain of maintaining it can cause unexpected stress.

Sheltered work and training facilities

Although these may seem the solution to all the problems of work, that is rarely the case. Sheltered work and training facilities usually operate the same standards regarding attendance, time-keeping and general reliability as would an employer. There may be some leniency at the outset, but this will not last long. The aim is to get people used to working, and all that that entails, not to provide an 'easy option'. Availability of places is extremely limited in either facility. Some sheltered workshops employ people over fairly lengthy periods of time, but others, and training facilities, expect people to move on to open employment after a comparatively short time. If the individual is not capable of that or is unable to find any suitable work, then he might find himself at home again with nothing gained.

Most of the training provided in such workshops is of a light industrial kind. There is little provision made for training in other sorts of work.

Leisure

One of the greatest problems that the unemployed sufferer has to face is boredom and what to do with his time. Many of the problems that apply to work apply to leisure activities too. An inability to concentrate for long, a general restlessness and a difficulty in socializing do not make enjoying leisure activities easy. Since, however, it is usually possible for the sufferer to leave if he feels anxious or unable to cope, he might be willing to at least try some activities.

Apathy and lack of initiative on the sufferer's part may be a major hurdle to be overcome before the sufferer can begin to do anything. The sufferer should be encouraged in any activities he had before he became ill or any in which he may now express an interest. If the sufferer is interested mainly in activities which he can pursue alone it might be worthwhile trying to get him involved in some club or organization to meet people as well. If he has a particular interest in, or knowledge of, something, he may feel more confident about meeting other people when he knows they have this in common and it will provide a topic of conversation.

Some sufferers may display a fleeting interest in a number of topics, or sometimes relatives can, in an attempt to find *something* the sufferer is interested in, give a casually expressed interest more importance than was intended. This can lead relatives into investing money in buying equipment, books or whatever, which are never used as the interest wanes. A modest outlay on materials or equipment is probably a better bet at the outset, together with as much support as the sufferer needs. More can be purchased later if the interest is sustained.

A word of warning in encouraging the sufferer's interests. Some sufferers get very involved in strange religious sects or philosophical groups. These need to be treated very warily. Even an interest in orthodox religious groups can get out of hand and become a matter of concern. Often the priest or minister of the church is the best person to consult, as he is experienced in dealing with a wide range of 'religious behaviour' and conversions, and can be surprisingly helpful and down-to-earth in suggesting what is, or is not, 'normal' in these circumstances. If you fear that your relative is coming under the influence of a group who you think could manipulate him to the group's advantage and his disadvantage, this should be discussed with the psychiatrist. Simply forbidding the sufferer from having anything to do with them or trying to talk him out of the association will only make him more determined to pursue it.

Sufferer-Domination of the Family

Sometimes domination of the family by the sufferer comes about fairly gradually and through indirect methods. His needs and wants are put first, the rest of the family being secondary. Thus, if the sufferer does not like other people visiting the house, friends and neighbours are no longer invited. If, for whatever reasons, the sufferer cannot be left alone, then his parents may never go out together, or they may never be able to take a holiday. The sufferer may be noisy at night, making it impossible for others to sleep.

Relatives as much as sufferers have their rights, which include some privacy, the need to do things alone or with someone other than the sufferer; they have a right to a life of their own. Arrangements should be made to make this possible. For example, another relative could stay with the sufferer for one evening, or people could drop in on a daily basis to allow parents to have a short holiday. In some instances, if the sufferer's condition warrants it, it may be possible for him to go into hospital for a week to allow relatives to have a much-needed break.

In some instances, though, the sufferer will resist all this and continue to make unacceptable demands. In such a case a confrontation is often necessary, when the family clearly and firmly tells the sufferer which of his demands or behaviours are unacceptable. The sufferer should be helped to understand how you, as relatives, feel and what you would like him to do instead. Again this should be clearly stated. Some bargaining will take place, but a compromise can often be reached. Maybe he does not want *any* visitors, and you want him to be sociable; a compromise might be that he will allow visitors without creating a scene, but you will allow him to stay in his room and not pressure him to join you. It is vital that the sufferer does not feel that the family is ganging-up against him and the issue should be explored from all points of view. Try to schedule such a confrontation at a time when everyone has a chance to know the discussion is going to take place and thus to think about it. Everyone should try to remain calm and controlled. It is *not* the time to hurl angry insults or accusations about. This means it is better not to have the discussion immediately after a confrontation of wills, when the sufferer has prevented someone from doing what they wanted. At such a time feelings will be less easily controlled.

A few sufferers seem to set out to cause trouble deliberately in the family, telling tales, passing on stories or confiding fears about other relatives' attitudes to him. Family members can find themselves set against each other without quite knowing how it has happened. Usually this will stem from the sufferer's own insecurities and the suspicions that form part of the illness. 'Stories' should always be checked and, if necessary, discrepancies pointed out to the sufferer, for example, 'Why did you tell me Dad said . . .?' Confrontation may be necessary from several people at a time to clear up some misunderstandings; but again the sufferer should not be made to feel that the family are united against him, that he is an outsider, or that anyone is trying to humiliate him. It may help to involve the sufferer more in family activities and to encourage him to feel part of the family circle. If necessary, and his behaviour does not change, refuse to discuss other relatives or friends with him, and tell him you will automatically discount anything he says.

Medication

Medication often becomes an issue of conflict between relative and sufferer, usually when the sufferer refuses to take the drugs prescribed for him. This tends to happen either at the beginning of the illness, when he refuses to believe he is ill, or when he is recovering and believes he does not need them any longer. If this is a problem it is worth confiding it to the doctor or community nurse since they will almost certainly try to convince the sufferer that he must stay on medication, and can watch for any deterioration in his condition.

When the sufferer refuses to take his medication, relatives might feel tempted to make sure he takes his drugs whether he knows it or not, and resort to crushing them to powder and adding them to his food. This is most inadvisable, since almost certainly the sufferer will find out what has been going on. The sufferer will, understandably, feel angry, hurt and betrayed. Even if this does not spill over into an aggressive outburst all trust will be lost between you and the sufferer, and ultimately it is a caring, trusting relationship that will benefit the sufferer most in the long run. Any tendency the sufferer may have towards paranoia will be intensified by such a course of action and will probably prove much harder to deal with in the future.

Sometimes long-term injections can get over the problem of having to take drugs daily, but this is an area where the psychiatrist's advice should be sought and taken.

Refusal to Accept Treatment

This problem most commonly shows itself in the form of refusal to take medication, discussed above. It may also mean that the sufferer will not see the GP or the psychiatrist, either when first ill or at time of relapse. How this is handled depends mainly on the particular views of the doctor involved, and how he or she interprets parts of the Mental Health Act (see Appendix).

Broadly speaking, someone can only be hospitalized against their will (sectioned) if they are of danger to themselves or others. 'Danger to themselves' would not normally be taken to mean that the sufferer will relapse if they stop taking their drugs. 'Danger to others' does not include making the family's life a misery. Psychiatrists vary considerably in their attitude to hospital admission, some of which depends on the availability of beds. As psychiatric hospitals are reduced, getting anyone admitted becomes more difficult. Admitting one person may only be possible by discharging another.

All this needs to be borne in mind when you consider how refusal to accept treatment is to be dealt with. A psychiatrist may want to admit someone, but can only do so if they agree, or when they become so ill they can be admitted involuntarily. Thus doctors as well as relatives are caught in the catch 22 of someone being too ill to manage easily at home, but not ill enough to be involuntarily admitted to hospital. Doctors differ in their ability to persuade reluctant patients into hospital, and sufferers differ in their persuadeability. Improved community services (see Chapter 5) may help this problem, as would the understanding that some sufferers need periods of asylum.

The problem of the sufferer refusing treatment can be compounded by the refusal of a GP or psychiatrist to make a home visit to assess the situation. They will often say this is because there is no point unless the patient is willing to co-operate. If the sufferer does not want to see the doctor they feel there is nothing they can do. This is difficult for relatives to understand, as well as being unfair on them. Chapter 11 discusses people who might be useful and how to approach them. Not being able to do anything for the patient is no excuse for abandoning the family.

There is no easy answer to the problem of a sufferer who refuses treatment. Accepting that the doctor's hands may be tied and they cannot do much may ease feelings of anger and bitterness on a personal level towards individuals. This, in turn, may make for an easier relationship, which may lead to greater trust and mutual respect, all of which makes searching for a solution that bit easier.

11.

GETTING HELP

Possibly one of the greatest difficulties experienced by sufferers and relatives is getting help, and the right kind of help, when they need it. A number of factors influence this problem, including the type of problem for which help is required, the co-operation of the sufferer, and the type of relationship both sufferer and relative have with the various professional agencies. Another important factor is making sure that the problem is directed to the right people to solve it. For example, if the issue concerns the sufferer's drugs, whether you or he thinks he is taking too much, or not enough, or you do not know what he is taking, or something has been changed and you want to know why, or you are worried about side-effects; then these questions must be directed to the psychiatrist (or GP where the GP is responsible for drugs). A medical doctor is the only person qualified to, and allowed to, prescribe drugs. Other people may be able to answer some of your questions, but may not be in a position to do so. For example, a nurse might be able to answer queries regarding the sufferer's medication, but be prevented from doing so by instructions from the psychiatrist.

Whom to Approach
Knowing who a person is and understanding what they do, and thus what you can reasonably expect of them, is important in getting the best out of the services available to you. To this end I have provided a list of people who can be of help, and a basic outline of what they can do. When looking for help, probably the best person to start with is whoever has been dealing with the problem, or that aspect of it, to date, and failure to do so may cause offence. If, however, someone is persistently unhelpful or refuses to take your problem seriously then you should seek help

elsewhere. This is easier in some cases than others. If, for example, your GP refuses to take your complaints about the sufferer's behaviour seriously you are entitled to ask for a referral to a psychiatrist (if you are not already seeing one). An alternative is to change your GP. Again, you are entitled to do this without giving any reason. If you choose this option, before selecting another GP try to find one who has a special knowledge of, and interest in, mental illness. Not all are trained and interested to the same degree. Other patients or relatives are often the best source of this advice, or anyone connected with a local mental health voluntary group.

If you are unhappy with your psychiatrist it is not always easy to change, especially consultants. If it is a junior doctor you are dissatisfied with, you can always ask to see the consultant and explain the problem to him. In most instances (unless there is clearcut evidence of negligence or malpractice) it is better not to make a complaint, even informally, since there is a regrettable tendency to close ranks and this may not help you or the sufferer.

If there is someone with whom you have a particularly good relationship, he can often be useful in putting you in touch with others, or interceding on your behalf. Remember, though, that there is a rigid hierarchy in medicine, and there is only a limited amount that those near the bottom can say to their superiors.

Much of this may sound as though I am suggesting that you pander to the professionals and try not to upset them. Where this *is* the case, it is with *your* best interests at heart. On the whole, you will get the best out of the system when you work *with* it and use it, rather than fight against it. A few people fight the system, or approach it in an unorthodox manner, with success, but many more try this and fail. Where they succeed it is because they are *one*; if everyone tried their tactics the system would not work at all. If you have someone on your side who knows the system and can help you work it to your best advantage, that way lies your greatest chance of success. This is not to say that you must sit back and accept the system as it stands, However, trying to change the system, to improve it, and getting help, are two *separate* issues and should be treated as such.

Who Does What

This is a list of the various professionals, who you may come across in hospitals and the community, involved in the case and treatment and rehabilitation of the sufferer.

Psychiatrist

This is a person who has a medical degree and has gone on to specialize in the treatment of mental disorders. The psychiatrist will be in charge of the case, that is, he has clinical responsibility for the care and treatment of the patient. Psychiatrists may be involved in a number of different kinds of therapies, but particularly physical therapies such as prescribing drugs and administering ECT. A group of psychiatrists work together and are headed by the Consultant. Under him are Senior Registrars and Registrars.

General Practitioner

This is someone who has a medical degree and has then gone on to specialize in family medicine. His knowledge of mental disorders and their treatment will be very variable and will largely depend on his interest. If you have a GP with little knowledge of, or interest in, mental illness it may well be worthwhile searching out one who has more. The GP will almost certainly refer someone he suspects to be schizophrenic to a psychiatrist. The GP can prescribe drugs and the responsibility for prescribing anti-psychotic drugs may revert to the GP when the patient is discharged from hospital or may remain with the hospital psychiatrist.

Clinical psychologist

This is a person who has a degree in psychology and has then gone on to do special training in clinical psychology. He may be involved in diagnosis and assessment, individual and group therapy and rehabilitation. Although he may use one or a combination of a variety of different therapy methods, the most commonly practised is behaviour therapy.

Social workers

Many social workers have a degree in a social studies or another subject and then have completed a postgraduate diploma course. Usually only those based in psychiatric hospitals or the psychiatric unit of a general hospital have any special interest in, knowledge of, or experience in, mental illness. Those who work in social service departments are less likely to be involved with psychiatric patients as such, working more with families and children.

Occupational therapist

Occupational therapists have received special training for working with both the physically ill and disabled and the mentally ill. Occupational therapy (or OT) is not only to fill time, but has more worthwhile objectives. Of two main types these will be either to find expression (and possibly release) through the creative process or to teach the individual the skills of daily living. Working with the former aim there may be associated specialist therapists, such as art, music or drama therapists.

Psychiatric nurse

Psychiatric nurses have undergone a special training to enable them to work with the mentally disturbed. Some may also be trained in general medicine. The nurse is possibly the most important person as far as the patient in hospital is concerned, because it is he or she who will see the patient most, and who is responsible for the day-to-day running of the ward. Nurses may take part in a number of ward therapy activities, including group sessions.

Community nurse

The community nurse will be psychiatrically trained as above, and in addition may have undergone a brief further training aimed at working in the community. In many hospitals it is the community nurse who supervises the medication of out-patients, often running special clinics for those on depot drugs, and who will check up when medication is missed. The number and type of home visits vary with hospital practice, staffing levels and types of problem, but they are often the first source of help in times of crisis or other worry to relatives or patient.

Disablement Resettlement Officer

The Disablement Resettlement Officer (or DRO) will be available to you either at your local Job Centre or through special visits at the hospital. He has special knowledge of local employment opportunities and what would be most suitable for the sufferer. The DRO may be able to put you in touch with sheltered employment opportunities or training schemes.

The DRO is also the person who makes decisions about who is eligible to register as disabled. A report is sent to the DRO from your doctor, and he may require you to see the Regional Medical

Officer. You must register for a period of one year, but can ask to be taken off the register at any time. The DRO should be able to give you advice about the advantages and disadvantages of being registered disabled. Although companies employing the disabled are required to have three per cent of their workforce registered as disabled, it is not necessarily a good thing to be registered.

Other Useful People
There are people outside the 'usual' channels of help and care who can provide help and support of various kinds; they may be particularly useful in helping you get what you want from the Health or Social Services.

Voluntary organizations
For many people the most support, help and advice they receive comes from voluntary organizations. Some of these are national, with local branches and groups, which may be specifically to do with schizophrenia or mental illness or some particular aspect, such as finances. Others may be locally organized groups to provide specific services, for example, social clubs.

Some useful groups are:

National Schizophrenia Fellowship,
   78-79 Victoria Road, Surbiton, Surrey, KT6 4WS.
National Schizophrenia Fellowship (Scotland),
   40 Shandwick Place, Edinburgh, Scotland.
The Northern Schizophrenia Fellowship,
   38 Collingwood Buildings, Collingwood Street,
   Newcastle-upon-Tyne, NE1 1GH.
The North-West Fellowship,
   10-12 Beaumont Street, Warrington, Cheshire, WA1 1DY.
MIND (National Association for Mental Health),
   22 Harley Street, London, W1N 1ED.
The Schizophrenia Association of Great Britain,
   Tgr, Twr, Llanfair Hall, Caernarvon, LL55 1TT, Gwynedd, Wales.

For queries concerning financial matters:

Disablement Income Group (DIG)
   152 Morrison Street, Edinburgh, EH3 8BY.

Ministers

Ministers, priests or vicars can often prove an important source of comfort and support to a family, not only to a relative or sufferer individually, but also as someone who may help a family come together to talk through problems. Because of their respected position and detachment from the family they can often be very helpful as intermediaries between relatives and other professionals, for example, in bringing home to the doctor the severity of the situation at a time of crisis when otherwise it might be seen as exaggeration by the relatives.

Solicitors

This group may be useful in helping to plan for the future by suggesting, for example, how sufferers might best be provided for in relatives' wills.

For patients who are compulsorily detained a solicitor may be invaluable in presenting the case at a tribunal (see Appendix) or in handling any complaints about treatment. In such cases a solicitor with a particular interest in the Mental Health Laws is vital. The Law Society can provide a list of suitable solicitors (as can MIND), if the local hospital cannot. In some cases legal aid will be available and this should be looked into.

Law Centres

Only found in larger cities, the various personnel at law centres, including solicitors, can often assist on legal aspects of problems. If necessary they might represent you in court or at a tribunal. Their services are free and they can give you details of legal aid. If you do not know where your nearest Law Centre is, you can find out from: The Law Centre Federation, 164 North Gower Street, London, NW1 2ND.

Citizens' Advice Bureau

The address of your local Citizens' Advice Bureau can be found in the telephone directory. Some have solicitors attached who give advice sessions; otherwise, if they cannot offer much advice themselves, they may be able to put you in touch with someone who can. All advice is free.

Members of Parliament

Links with your MP are important, not only on an individual basis, but particularly for local and national affairs. Canvass him about any legislation to be discussed that will affect mental patients. For individual problems you can attend the constituency surgery. If you are representing a local group you could also make contact with his secretary and research assistant. Get to know the 'team' and build a relationship with them. Let them know of your group's goals and invite the MP to meet the group.

Local Councillors
Canvass these on local or individual issues, particularly on provision of community care (or lack of it!). They hold local surgeries at which you can discuss issues. Again, if you are a member of a group let them know about it and invite them to come and speak to you. Make contact with the person on the Council responsible for Social Services and make him aware of your views on the help available from social services locally (either as an individual or a group).

Community Health Councils
These represent the patient's interests and rights in relation to the National Health Service. Some run advice centres and should be able to clear up points for you on patients' rights. Again, they are useful people to contact from a group and to invite as speakers.

Getting the Most Out of Your Doctor
Since even getting an appointment to see a psychiatrist or other professional is often extremely difficult, you want to make the most of the opportunity once you get it. Most of these suggestions will apply to other groups of people, including solicitors and MPs. Although doctors are used to seeing people who are distressed and in an emotional state, and should be trained to deal with this, it does not always follows that they do cope well. Although I would agree that many need to improve in those areas, for you to get the most out of *your* doctor *now, you* are going to have to be the one to make the changes.

1. Be clear in your own mind what the problem is and what you are complaining about. The jumbled collection of upsets and difficult behaviour from the patient, dissatisfaction with help received and your own problems and difficulties in coping which is poured out makes it hard for both you and the doctor

to really know what is going on and where your priorities lie. It is all too easy to concentrate on trivialities and miss the more important issues. You need to know exactly what it is you want to say.

2. To this end *write it down*. Just put down anything and everything that is bothering you in one long list. As you write, one idea will trigger off another. Do not worry at this stage that it is all a jumble.

3. Once you have got your thoughts and feelings down, then put them under *headings*. These might include problems the sufferer has, problems you have dealing with the sufferer, difficulties you have in coping generally and concerns about your own health, family problems resulting from the sufferer's illness and difficulties you are experiencing in getting help. There may be others appropriate to your circumstances. These headings are not rigid, so do not worry about any overlap. If you think his condition is deteriorating you might want to list this with approximate dates, e.g., a month ago he could . . ., now he cannot.

4. Having got these lists, you now need to put them into order of *priority.* This should be priority as *you* see it and not what might appear to others as the most important problem. An argument or seemingly trivial behavioural quirk that happens every day may cause more disruption at home than an apparently more serious 'symptom' that either happens rarely or does not affect anyone else. Even if you do not give it to the doctor, keep with you a list of past hospital admissions, treatments (if you know them), people seen and other similarly relevant information, and you can prompt the doctor if necessary.

5. When you have this list of priorities give it to the psychiatrist or GP. If you think it would help, send it ahead of time to the doctor, together with a note of when you are going to see him and what you want to discuss. If the doctor is unable to help in certain areas ask for referrals to other people, e.g., a psychologist or social worker, or even just for suggestions of who to contact.

6. Take paper and a pen with you when you see the doctor and write down his suggestions, either for who to contact or what to do. Most people find it hard to remember what their doctor tells them and if you are at all upset or anxious then

remembering anything is even harder. Writing things down also prevents confusion when you are told a lot of things at once.

7. Do not go into the doctor with a list of demands of things that he *must* do. This is likely to put anyone's back up, and especially if you are demanding certain drugs or changes in them then many doctors will react badly to what they see as someone trying to teach them their job. It is possible, however, to point out 'He never did . . . before he was on . . .' 'When he took . . . then . . . was much better' or even '. . . seems worse since his medication was changed,' and then follow this up with the question, 'Could there be a connection?' You are offering all the information you can about the sufferer's condition, and most doctors will recognize that you see all kinds of things at home that they do not. This information helps the doctor to make the best decisions concerning the sufferer's care.

8. It might seem that I am trying to make things easy for the doctor, and to some extent this is true, since then you are likely to get a better service from him. But that does not mean that doctors should be allowed to get away with doing nothing. You must be *persistent*. Keep telling him that the problems are the same, do not let him think that things are improving when they are not. If a GP is very unhelpful then change him. If a psychiatrist will not see you, ask to see someone else. If necessary contact your local Health Council for advice about your rights and how to pursue them. Keep asking for help, reiterating problems, until you find someone who will take them seriously and either help you or direct you to the people who can. Persist, where possible, and for as long as possible, but persist politely.

9. Keep records of your contacts with doctors, copies of letters you send and so on; then you can confront a doctor with details of how long a problem has persisted and what you have done about it should this become necessary. This is more to give you confidence in saying 'I have spoken to you about this three times before' when the doctor looks blank, than it is for any other purpose.

Confidentiality

There is one vital point to bear in mind when discussing the sufferer with his doctor which is that the doctor's first responsibility is to his patient, and that includes keeping what he is told confidential. He can only discuss certain aspects of the case with you with his patient's permission and that includes details of treatment and medication. You might explain how not knowing some things makes it difficult for you to care for the sufferer on a day-to-day basis, but recognize that there are some things the doctor simply cannot ethically discuss with you. You should, however, be given details of discharge, when the sufferer is being discharged back to your care.

12.

PREVENTION OF SCHIZOPHRENIA

Preventing schizophrenia is probably of concern to everyone involved with the problem but, as in everything else to do with schizophrenia, it is easier said than done. Prevention means different things to different people, from preventing new cases to minimizing the risk of relapse in someone in whom schizophrenia has already developed. The former is not possible, the latter may be.

Preventing Schizophrenia

Although we know that it is extremely likely that the potential to develop schizophrenia is inherited, this is not the same as saying that the illness itself is inherited. Chapter 4 discusses the possibilities of genetic transmission. However, genetic counselling is not generally available to either schizophrenic sufferers or those with schizophrenia in the family. The closer the blood tie to the schizophrenic patient the higher the risk of transmitting schizophrenia, but it must be remembered that these risks themselves are fairly low. Even where one parent is schizophrenic the likelihood of an offspring becoming schizophrenic is about ten to fifteen per cent. Where both parents are schizophrenic there is a much higher risk of a child becoming schizophrenic, possibly even forty to fifty per cent.

It should be borne in mind that even in a child who has the potential to develop schizophrenia it might be possible to prevent its appearance.

Preventing the Development of Schizophrenia

The most that can be done here is to promote a healthy environment in which the child can grow up happy and secure. It is probably equally important not to go too far in the opposite direction and become over-protective and smothering. Although the schizophrenic individual responds badly to stress, to function normally in the world the growing child needs to be exposed to everyday frustrations and stresses, and needs to learn how to cope successfully with them. A danger in trying to protect a possible schizophrenic may result in someone who would not have become schizophrenic developing other problems.

Preventing Relapse

It is once we move into the area of trying to minimize relapse in those who have already shown signs of schizophrenia that we seem to be on somewhat firmer ground. Some of these points have already been mentioned and can be summarized here.

1. *The emotional atmosphere of the family.* This has been discussed in Chapter 7 and relates to high expressed emotion. Maintaining a calm non-critical position whilst providing love, support and acceptance is important.
2. *Medication.* If the psychiatrist thinks the sufferer will do well on medication then he should take it regularly as prescribed. If he *does* do well, then it should be continued: this is *not* a sign to stop!
3. *Time away from the family.* If possible, the sufferer should be away from the family for at least part of each day. This becomes vital if the family atmosphere is very strained.
4. *Life events.* If there are big changes in the sufferer's life then the subsequent three to four weeks may be a particularly vulnerable time. The sufferer may need more support, less demands made on him and possible changes in his medication.

These four suggestions are the most important, with the most clear evidence to support them. Other useful suggestions may be:

5. Try to maintain good diet habits and regular nourishment.
6. Try to maintain (or begin) some form of regular exercise. This may only need to be very gentle in some cases, but the sufferer should not sit passively all day.
7. Try to maintain or establish good sleeping habits and the normal cycle of being up during the day and sleeping at night, rather than the reverse.
8. Try to maintain normal family relationships and contacts.

Include the sufferer when and where possible, without too much pressure to join in.

9. Try to maintain social contacts and friends.
10. Try to maintain or establish interests, hobbies and things to do that stop the sufferer sinking into apathy and withdrawal.

APPENDIX: THE LEGAL POSITION

The legal position of the schizophrenic person, in relation to treatment and his rights as both a patient and an individual, can be quite complex and depends not only on the circumstances surrounding the sufferer, but also where he lives. The law in Scotland and Northern Ireland is different in some respects to that in England and Wales. This chapter can only look briefly at some of the more common things patients and families want to know about the law, particularly regarding admission. Further information is available from the voluntary organizations, or a comprehensive look at the new legislation is available in a book produced by MIND — *A Practical Guide to Mental Health Law* by Larry Gostin.

The Mental Health Act 1983 made a number of changes to the previous 1959 Act, most importantly to give patients greater protection regarding the use of compulsory treatment or admission. The following points regarding the law refer to England and Wales.

Who Does the Act Apply To?

The Act uses the term 'mental disorder' which is then defined as 'mental illness, arrested or incomplete development of mind, psychopathic disorder and any other disorder or disability of mind'. Whilst this covers a very broad range of behaviour the Act is careful to exclude from mental disorder 'promiscuity or other immoral conduct, sexual deviancy or dependence on alcohol or drugs'.

Mental illness and severe mental impairment are classified as *major disorders,* and therefore do *not* usually require to be *treatable* for a person to be detained compulsorily. Mental impairment and psychopathic disorders are regarded as *minor* and must be *treatable* if a person is to be compulsorily admitted and detained. Schizophrenia falls under the legal definition of mental illness.

Voluntary or Informal Patient Status
Over ninety per cent of patients have 'informal' status. This means that the patient is not *unwilling* to be admitted, rather than that they have necessarily asked for admission. The patient can leave hospital at any time subject to *holding powers*.

Holding power
A *nurse* can hold a patient, who wants to leave hospital, for six hours — if he believes it necessary for the health and safety of the patient, or for the protection of others, and it is not possible immediately to have the doctor attend. This has to be recorded in writing on the prescribed form. Once the doctor has arrived the nurse's holding power lapses.

A *doctor* can hold a patient for seventy-two hours when he considers that an application for compulsory admission 'ought to be made'. A report has to be made to the hospital managers. The nurse's six hours counts as part of the seventy-two. A doctor can use this power to detain *any* in-patient; the nurse can only use it to detain an in-patient being treated for mental disorder.

Compulsory Admission
The types of admission described here are under Part II of the Act and patients so detained may be described as 'Part II' patients.

Emergency Admission for Assessment (Section 4)
There must be an 'urgent necessity' for the patient to be admitted because the normal procedure would involve 'undesirable delay'. The admission lasts for seventy-two hours and must be recommended by one doctor, with application being made by either an approved social worker or the nearest relative, who has seen the patient within the last twenty-four hours. For further detention an application for admission for assessment must be made.

Admission for Assessment (Section 2)
This lasts for twenty-eight days and must be recommended by two doctors, with application being made by either an approved

social worker or the nearest relative, who has seen the patient within the last two weeks. Again, detention is necessary in the interest of the patient's own health or safety or to protect others.

A social worker can make application for admission for assessment *without* the nearest relative's knowledge or consent, but must 'take such steps as are practicable' to inform the relative. The nearest relative can order the patient's discharge, or the patient can apply to a Mental Health Review Tribunal for discharge.

Admission for Treatment (Section 3)

The order lasts for six months, renewable for a further six months and then renewable yearly. Recommendation for admission must be made by two doctors and an application by an approved social worker or nearest relative. The nearest relative can make a *formal objection* to this by notifying that social worker or the local authority social services department. The social worker *must* consult the nearest relative *unless* this is not 'reasonably practicable' or such consultation would involve 'unreasonable delay'. If the relative does object, the social worker can make application to the county court to *displace* the nearest relative.

Admission for treatment can be made for both in-patients and those outside hospital. The person's mental disorder must be of a degree or nature which makes hospital treatment appropriate, and in the case of minor disorders this treatment is likely to either alleviate the condition or prevent deterioration. This does not apply to major disorders. Lastly, it must be seen that such treatment is necessary for the health or safety of the patient, or for the protection of others, and that it is not possible to provide such treatment unless the patient is detained under this section.

The treatability requirement is applicable in *all* cases of renewal except in cases of major disorder where a person who is 'untreatable' is also 'unlikely to be able to care for himself, to obtain the care which he needs or to guard himself against serious exploitation'.

Mentally Disordered Persons Found in Public Places (Section 136)

The police can take a person who they believe to be both suffering from mental disorder and 'in immediate need of care or control' to a 'place of safety'. They can detain him there for seventy-two hours so that he can be examined by a doctor and interviewed by an approved social worker and necessary arrangements made for care and/or treatment.

Warrant to Search For and Remove Patients (Section 135)

A person who is believed to be suffering from mental disorder can be detained for seventy-two hours if there is 'reasonable cause' to suspect that he is being ill-treated, neglected or not kept under proper control, or is living alone and unable to care for himself. An approved social worker must lay information, on oath, before a Justice of the Peace; then a police constable, together with a doctor and approved social worker, can enter the patient's premises, by force if necessary, and then remove him to a place of safety.

Guardianship

The patient who is over sixteen years old must be suffering from a mental disorder which makes his reception into guardianship necessary. This is defined as being in the interests of the welfare of the patient, or for the protection of others. A recommendation is made by two doctors and the application by an approved social worker or the nearest relative who must have seen the patient within the last fourteen days. The same restrictions apply to the social worker as they do under admission for treatment.

The guardian is either the local social service authority or a person accepted by the authority for the area in which the guardian lives. Guardianship is for six months, which is then renewable for a further six months, and yearly thereafter.

The powers of the guardian enable him to require the patient to live in a specified place, and to attend specified places for the purpose of medical treatment, occupation, education or training. The guardian can also require that access to the patient is available to any doctor, approved social worker, or other person specified by the guardian.

Patients under a Guardianship order enjoy the same rights as informal patients and they cannot be compelled by the guardian to take part in any treatment to which they do not consent.

Criminal Proceedings and Admission to Hospital

These apply to very few people. It is possible for a court to send or remand a person to hospital for a medical report, to remand to hospital for treatment and for an interim hospital order to be made to determine whether a hospital order would be suitable. This means that a person can be examined in hospital, and even treated for a limited time, before the court makes a final decision on the case. Since these requirements mean that that the NHS must make provision for such referrals, it will take some time before the Act is implemented.

People in prison can be transferred to hospital if their condition warrants such a move and change in status.

Discharge from Hospital

Discharge means slightly different things depending on how the patient is detained. But it always has to do with whether there is any justifiable reason for continuing to detain a person, rather than whether the patient was lawfully admitted and detained in the first place.

Discharge by the hospital

When a patient is in hospital he can be discharged by the Reponsible Medical Officer (RMO), who is the doctor in charge of his case, or by the hospital managers.

Discharge by the nearest relative

Unless a patient has been admitted as the result of an emergency admission the nearest relative has the right to order the discharge of a patient. If the patient is under a detention order for either treatment or assessment the nearest relative must give the hospital manager seventy-two hours notice, in writing, of the intention to discharge. Within this time the doctor can then give a report to the managers in support of continued detention. The patient must be 'likely to act in a manner dangerous to other persons or to himself'. If this is done then the relative's discharge order is void. The relative can make no further order for six months unless the patient has been admitted for treatment, when the relative has twenty-eight days in which to appeal to a Mental Health Review Tribunal to request the patient's discharge.

Mental Health Review Tribunal

Mental Health Review Tribunals (MHRTs) are made up of lawyers, doctors and lay people; they are independent bodies and they hear applications by patients or relatives in respect of patients detained in hospital or under guardianship. They are concerned with continued detention and discharge, *not* with patients' complaints.

Legal aid is available for the patient who is to be represented by a solicitor at the MHRT.

Who can apply?

The patient can apply within fourteen days if admitted for assessment, or within the first six months of admission for treatment, or reception into guardianship, then again during the next six months and thereafter yearly.

The nearest relative can only apply if the doctor in charge has issued a report to the hospital managers which has stopped the relative from discharging the patient. This application must be made within twenty-eight days of this happening.

The Secretary of State for Social Services can refer a patient detained under Part II of the Act at any time, as can the Home Secretary for restricted patients. Hospital managers must refer a patient admitted for treatment within six months, and subsequently every three years.

Consent to Treatment

Regulations about consent to treatment (Part IV of the 1983 Act) are complicated, and apply only to patients who are 'liable to be detained' (except those under emergency admission, a nurse's or doctor's holding power or police power). Informal patients and those detained for seventy-two hours or less *have the right to refuse treatment* under common law.

Consent under Common Law

Consent may be given by a patient either directly, through speech or in writing, or it can be implied by the patient's behaviour. Consent can be withdrawn at any time.

Consent has three main elements:

1. *Information* — The patient must be told what the treatment is and what it hopes to achieve, and also about any *serious* side-effects, but not necessarily minor risks. The patient is entitled to ask for more information and to obtain truthful answers.
2. *Competency* — The patient must be able to understand what he is being told about the nature and purpose of the treatment. This is a grey area, since there are severely ill informal patients who are unable to give consent.
3. *Voluntariness* — The patient must give his consent voluntarily, without coercion, unreasonable influence being exerted, or deceit.

Consent for Treatment given under Part IV of the Act

Some treatment categories cannot be given without specific consent to Part IV patients.

These are:

1. Psychosurgery and sex hormone implant treatment.
2. ECT, and medication *after* it has been administered for three months. In this case consent means:

a)   consent (as described under common law) being verified in writing by a doctor (*not* the doctor in charge) and two others (*not* doctors) appointed by the Mental Health Act Commission.

b)   A second opinion (doctor appointed by the MHAC) has to certify in writing that treatment should be given, 'having regard to the likelihood of the treatment alleviating or preventing a deterioration of the patient's condition'.

c)   This doctor must *consult* with two other people on the therapeutic team, one a nurse and the other neither a nurse nor a doctor.

For other types of treatment for mental disorder, which includes nursing, if a patient falls within the parameters of Part IV of the Act then the patient can be treated without consent or a second opinion.

Urgent treatment

Treatment can be given without consent or a second opinion if it is immediately necessary to save the patient's life. It can be given to prevent a serious deterioration if it is not irreversible or hazardous, to alleviate serious suffering on the part of the patient, or if it is immediately necessary and represents the minimum necessary to stop the patient from either being a danger to himself or to others or behaving violently.

Nearest Relative

By nearest relative the Act means:

husband or wife
son or daughter
father or mother
brother or sister
grandparent
grandchild

uncle or aunt
nephew or niece

The *nearest* relative is the first person on this list. If there are two relatives of the same standing, for example a son *and* a daughter, the *eldest* is deemed to be the nearest relative. If, however, the patient 'ordinarily resides with, or is cared for' by one or more of his relatives, or was living with them immediately before he was admitted to hospital, then that relative(s) is usually given precedence over the others.

Non-relatives may be considered 'nearest relative' in some special circumstances. If the patient has lived with someone as husband or wife for six months, then that person is treated as the patient's spouse and is the nearest relative. If the patient has lived with a non-relative, but not as husband and wife, for five years, then that person is legally considered a relative, but not necessarily the nearest relative.

Powers of the nearest relative
The nearest relative can make applications for compulsory admission to hospital, for guardianship, to order discharge and to require an approved social worker to consider making an application for compulsory admission.

Displacement by County Court
If the patient has no nearest relative, or if that person is incompetent, or unreasonably objects to an application for compulsory admission, or discharges the patient without due regard for the welfare of the patient or the public, then the County Court can appoint another person to act as nearest relative. *Any* of the patient's relatives, or the person he lived with before admission, or an approved social worker can apply to the County Court for a displacement order.

Other Aspects of Law
The Law also describes the Mental Health Act Commission and its powers, the rights of the patient in hospital, the patient's rights in the community and the management of the patient's property and affairs. Details of these, and further explanations of the Act, can be obtained from MIND, Law Centres, Citizens Advice Bureaux or the National Schizophrenia Fellowship.

The Law can be very complicated and will mainly only be of concern if a patient is being compulsorily detained, has a guardianship order, or is unable to manage his own affairs. Expert advice should be sought in all cases.

FURTHER READING

There are endless books written about schizophrenia, but of these comparatively few that explain to the non-schizophrenic what it is like to have schizophrenia.

The following are a few of the case histories which are more or less easily available and help us understand the schizophrenic experience from various viewpoints. Most are biography, one or two are novels. Not all of these books are currently in print, but should be available from the library.

There are a few points to remember when reading these books.

1. Some of these people would not always be diagnosed schizophrenic — in particular there are differences between America and Britain. Particularly in novels the term schizophrenic may be used very loosely.
2. Some of the methods of treatment may now be out of date — care needs to be taken in determining when something happened, e.g. ECT is uncommon for schizophrenics now, unless the person is also very depressed, but was more common in the 1950s and 1960s.
3. America and Britain have different approaches to treatment — particularly when considering some of the 'fringe' areas of private medicine in America. Psychoanalysis, for example, is not common in Britain, is virtually unobtainable on the NHS and of no proven use in schizophrenia. Likewise megavitamin therapy is not available here, and note that many sufferers who attribute their improvement/recovery to this are *also* taking standard medication *which is* available and used in Britain.
4. A final point is that most stories tell of success, particularly where the book is autobiography, and although this is encouraging it does not necessarily mean that the outcome of all is so good, or even that such treatments will help many.

Mary Barnes and Joseph Berke, *Mary Barnes — Two Accounts of a Journey Through Madness* (MacGibbon and Kee, 1971). Also published by Penguin.
The story of a schizophrenic breakdown told by the sufferer and her psychiatrist. Tremendous detail of breakdown and her feelings and experiences during this. It describes an unusual approach to therapy, not widely used or accepted, in a residential centre in London set up by R.D. Laing. The emphasis is on 'living through' the episodes and using them to enrich the individual's experience. Interesting because of the insights into the approach, the problems of the psychiatrist and how the approach is not as easy or straightforward as it is sometimes presented. An interesting and unusual account, but not 'standard' in its approach by any means.

Terra Ford, *Schizophrenia Cured* (Canadian Schizophrenic Foundation), 1979
Story of a young nun's schizophrenia told by the sufferer. Includes also a brief explanation of the orthomolecular approach to schizophrenia and megavitamin and controlled diet therapy, an approach not used here.

Hannah Green, *I Never Promised You a Rose Garden* (Victor Gollancz, 1964). Numerous editions in Pan Books.
This is possibly the best-known novel about a young schizophrenic girl, although it is possible that she would not now be diagnosed schizophrenic. Life in a private mental hospital in the early 1960s is portrayed, together with treatment by psychotherapy. It gives a good insight into a private delusional and hallucinatory world.
    A film has been made of the book which is helpful to show that what the sufferer sees is 'real' to her.

F. McDonald. ed. H.R. Rollin, *A Tragedy of Schizophrenia — The Wife's Tale* (N.S.F. Publication)
The description of a schizophrenic breakdown by the wife of a sufferer, including difficulties and frustrations in dealing with the medical and legal professions, told as a series of letters between the participants.

John Newfeld, *Lisa, Bright and Dark* (Signet Books, 1969)
This novel is the story of a sixteen year old schoolgirl who is losing

touch with reality and is helped and supported by three friends until they can convince the adults around them of her need for help. Her parents refuse to accept that she is ill or needs help and the other adults act helpless. The story is told by one of the young girls. It is of some help in understanding the problems of teenage behaviour and the distinction between 'a phase she is going through' and illness.

Barbara O'Brien, *Operators and Things: The Inner Life of a Schizophrenic* (Abacus Books, 1976. First published in USA 1958) The story of an acute a schizophrenic episode (and subsequent recovery) told by the sufferer, a young American girl. Interesting because she describes her delusional beliefs and the way they affected her life and it makes otherwise inexplicable behaviour comprehensible, indeed normal.

Brenda Lucas Ogdon and Michael Kerr, *Virtuoso. The Story of John Ogdon* (Hamish Hamilton Ltd, 1981) The story of the British concert pianist John Ogden, written by his wife. It describes their life from being students to the present — quite a lot of attention and detail being given on his rise to fame — and goes on to describe his breakdown, including suicide attempts, recovery, relapse and recovery, etc. His problems are first diagnosed as being due to a schizophrenic breakdown and later to manic depression. Some description of wife's difficulties and problems.

David Reed, *Anna* (Secker and Warburg, 1976) The diary of the husband of a schizophrenic woman. He describes her feelings and experiences through his eyes, as well as his own feelings and problems and difficulties with their children. He describes the difficulties in getting good, sensible treatment and the final tragedy.

Flora Rheta Schreiber, *Sybil* (First published in 1973 in USA. Published in Great Britain by Penguin — several reprints.) This is the story of a woman who is a 'split personality' as told by someone well known to her psychoanalyst and who becomes well known to the subject. Split personality is very rare, and not at all the same thing as schizophrenia and I include it here to show the difference. The girl's mother is described as schizophrenic and there are some descriptions of her and her problems. It has been made into a television film.

Mark Vonnegut, *The Eden Express* (Praeger Pub. Inc., 1975)
The story of a schizophrenic breakdown told by the sufferer, a young man. He describes his feelings and experiences and the book is interesting as it is set against a 'hippy, drop-out' background and commune. Despite his friends' willingness to try to keep him with them they are eventually forced to seek traditional medical help. Describes therapy not normally available in Britain, in positive terms, *but note* that he is on the major drugs used in Britain *as well*.

Mary Jane Ward, *The Snake Pit* (Random House, 1946. Signet Books 1977)
The horrifying story (novel) of a young woman's incarceration in an asylum in the 1940s, including an account of all the old, 'tortuous' types of treatment, *now out of date*. There is some good insight into the schizophrenic thinking behind both normal and abnormal behaviour.

Self-help books
Paul Bebbington and Liz Kuipers, *Living With Mental Illness* (Souvenir Press, 1987)
This book describes both schizophrenia and manic-depressive illness and, as well as describing symptoms and causes, looks at ways of managing the problems. A useful book.

Clare Creer and John Wing, *Schizophrenia at Home* (National Schizophrenia Fellowship. Second edition 1988)
This is a revamped edition of a 1974 book put out by the National Schizophrenia Fellowship. Relatives describe in their own words how schizophrenia has affected the family and how they cope. Particularly useful for reassuring you that you're not alone.

E. Fuller Torrey, *Surviving Schizophrenia. A Family Manual.* (Harper and Row. Revised edition 1988)
This fairly long book takes a comprehensive look at schizophrenia, its symptoms, causes and treatment, as well as sections on history, management, and legal and ethical issues. It is a useful book.

INDEX